The Four Filters
Invention
of
Warren Buffett & Charlie Munger

by Bud Labitan

D1564669

The Four Filters Invention of Warren Buffett and Charlie Munger

Two Friends Transformed Behavioral Finance

By Bud Labitan

ISBN 978-0-6152-4129-6

The use of the quotes in this book has been granted by Mr. Warren
Buffett, but this does not imply any endorsement of this book.

TABLE OF CONTENTS

TABLE OF CONTENTS

ACKNOWLEDGMENTS

I am grateful to my family and friends for their careful reading of the manuscript. Thanks to Janine Rueth, Rosemary Rueth, Brett Baker, JT Loudermilk, and Rick Mayhew for their keen reading and careful critique. Thanks to Bakul Lalla for generating the *"Effective Yield of a Bargain Purchase after 10-years Chart"* seen at the end of this book. It is definitely a revelation.

How many of us know that "Alma mater" is Latin for "nourishing mother"? Thanks to the Faculty and Staff of Purdue University Calumet's School of Management in Hammond, Indiana. You have fine MBA programs that just keep getting better.

The use of the quotes in this book has been granted by Mr. Warren Buffett, but this does not imply any endorsement of my book.

Bud Labitan
budlabitan@aol.com
www.frips.com

INTRODUCTION

How do we improve and optimize our investing decision making? We can use the Four Filters Invention of Warren E. Buffett and Charles T. Munger. Their rational four filters investing process help us eliminate many inferior investing prospects, and they help us find high-quality winning investments. Their logical steps to evaluating a business, its products, its competitive position, its managers, and its intrinsic value, provide us with a tested and effective set of tools. The Four Filters are a search for: "Understandable first-class businesses, with enduring competitive advantages, accompanied by first-class managements, available at a bargain price."[1]

In my view, Warren Buffett and Charlie Munger invented an investing formula that is underappreciated by the business and academic communities. The Four Filters developed by Warren Buffett and Charlie Munger is an amazing intellectual achievement in both practical and Behavioral Finance. The Four Filters are a remarkable and important set of steps used by the world's greatest investors for finding high quality investments. The Four Filters function as an effective time-tested focusing formula for investing success. They serve as a very useful guide for assessing intrinsic value and sensible price. They help us frame our investing process correctly, and they help us prevent foolish and costly investing losses. Using this process, you and I can become better investors. We can improve the way we think about businesses.

This innovative formula uses qualitative factors as well as quantitative factors to help us find and insure a good stock or whole business for investment. It will raise the odds of investing success. This book restates many of the writings and talks of Buffett and Munger using their words to tell a story from their perspective, as well as from my viewpoint.

This story is about two good friends who smartly changed the world of investing and invented a thoughtful and effective process. They made a lot of money for themselves and for their shareholders. For me and for you, there is another treasure hidden in these words: how to improve and optimize our decision making process. This is also a story about exercising self-discipline. Look to the future and think clearly for yourself. Be open to new ideas from wise people. Study the past, and learn from it. As Ben Graham said in the introduction of his book, *The Intelligent Investor*: "No statement is more true and better applicable to Wall Street than the famous warning of Santayana: "Those who do not remember the past are condemned to repeat it." This book is about one smart way to frame a decision process using sound principles.

How do we develop a better understanding of a business, its products, its present, its earnings, and its future? Charlie Munger said, "We read a lot. I don't know anyone who's wise who doesn't read a lot. But that's not enough: You have to have a temperament to grab ideas and do sensible things."[2] Over the years, I have read all of the Letters to Shareholders of Berkshire Hathaway, most of the books and articles about Warren Buffett, his teacher Benjamin Graham, and his business partner Charlie Munger. Having listened to many hours of audio lectures and interviews, I have been consistently interested in how Warren Buffett and Charlie Munger "frame" an investment decision, and how they find a winning investment prospect. This book is a story about the rational four filter process that help Buffett and Munger make better investing decisions. In the words of Charlie Munger, "You have to understand the odds and have the discipline to bet only when the odds are in your favor."[3]

Warren Buffett has written about the Four Filters in several ways. This behavioral sequence is always similar: **"Charlie and I look for companies that have a) a business we understand; b) favorable long-term economics; c) able and trustworthy management; and d) a sensible price tag."**[4] While Charlie Munger has described the process as getting into high quality businesses, Warren Buffett has also phrased the Four Filter process in this slightly different way: **"When buying companies or common stocks, we look for understandable first-class businesses, with enduring competitive advantages, accompanied by first-class managements, available at a bargain price."**[5]

After devoting hours of thinking time into their investing ideas and guiding principles[6], I felt like a man who stumbled upon hidden treasure in the middle of his back yard. I rediscovered a simple sequence called the Four Filters! They were there all the time.

In the 2003 Berkshire Hathaway annual meeting, a man asked Warren Buffett this question: "Could you just take us thru your filter process when it comes to, selecting a company?" Warren Buffett answered, "It's a question of a. Can I understand it?...if it

makes it thru that filter…b. Does it have some kind of sustainable long-term competitive advantage…" If it makes it thru that filter…How do I feel about the management in terms of, their ability and honesty?.. and if it makes it thru that filter,…What's the price?... And if it gets it thru all four filters, I sign my name to the check."

These ideas sound so simple. Many people hear them at the Berkshire Hathaway annual meeting in Omaha each year. Yet, few people have stopped to think about the importance and usefulness of each individual filter. As a formula, the Four Filters function as a set of "Investing Best Practices." They help us develop better "self-control." They force us to focus on "Wonderful Businesses."[7] They function as a smart targeting system steering us with clear goals. And, using the Four Filters, promotes investing "self-discipline." This book will also unveil how the Four Filters are a significant intellectual achievement in Behavioral Finance.

The checklist nature of these Four Filters serve as a logical and sensible justification mechanism. A checklist can serve to confirm or disconfirm evidence. Like pilots who use checklist prior to flying, the Four Filters help us frame a rational investment decision. Charlie Munger believes in using checklist routines to help us avoid a lot of errors. These errors occur because our human brains are wired to find shortcuts, or what Munger calls "shortcut types of approximations." Charlie Munger said: "The main antidotes to miscues from Availability-Misweighing Tendency often involve procedures, including the use of checklists, which are almost always helpful."[8] At the USC Law School Commencement speech in 2007, he said: "You should have all of this elementary wisdom, and you should go through a mental checklist in order to use it. There is no other procedure that will work as well."[9] To be fair, many other great investors used quality checklists to earn profits. And, many other great investors contributed "Best Practices" to the art of effective investing. Later in this book, we see the contributions of several investing thought leaders.

Do you have a "Happy Zone?" The Four Filters serve to increase the probability of investment success by defining "the right ball to hit." Here is Warren Buffett's Ted Williams analogy: "I put heavy weight on certainty. Use probability in your favor and avoid risk. It's not risky to buy securities at a fraction of what they are worth. Don't gamble. You're dealing with a lot of silly people in the marketplace; it's like a great big casino, and everyone else is boozing. Watch for unusual circumstances. Great investment opportunities come around when excellent companies are surrounded by unusual circumstances that cause the stock to be misappraised. In appraising the odds, Ted Williams explained how he increased his probability of hitting: "My argument is, to be a good hitter, you've got to get a good ball to hit. It's the first rule in the book."

This book concentrates on the four sequential filters that can help us become better and more skillful investment decision makers. This book trims "all the lean beef" into five chapters: "the Four Filter chapters and a summarizing chapter." The final summary chapter will tie the filters together and demonstrate why these filters work to maximize the probability of investing success from both a mathematical and a practical point of view.

So, how were these Four Filters developed? Over the course of their investing experiences, Warren Buffett and Charlie Munger have had many discussions about the qualities of bad, good, and mediocre businesses. Keep in mind that Charlie Munger believes wisdom acquisition is a moral duty.[10] The Four Filters seem to have evolved from these discussions and their early business and investing experiences. Interestingly, the 1977 Letter to

Shareholders of Berkshire Hathaway is the earliest one listing the Four Filters. It is also the earliest letter posted at the company's website: (http://www.berkshirehathaway.com). This Four Filters Formula was presented in this form: "We select our marketable equity securities in much the same way we would evaluate a business for acquisition in its entirety. **We want the business to be (1) one that we can understand, (2) with favorable long-term prospects, (3) operated by honest and competent people, and (4) available at a very attractive price.**"[11]

Charlie Munger said that once they had gotten over the hurdle of recognizing that a thing (business) could be a bargain based on quantitative measures that would have horrified Ben Graham, they started thinking about better businesses. Their results show the bulk of the billions earned at Berkshire Hathaway have come from the better businesses. Munger described their system this way: "We came to this notion of finding a mispriced bet and loading up when we were very confident that we were right. So we're way less diversified. And I think our system is miles better."[12]

Warren Edward Buffett was born August 30, 1930, in Omaha, Nebraska. He is regarded as one of the world's greatest stock market and business investors. He is the largest shareholder and CEO of Berkshire Hathaway. Warren Buffett was greatly influenced by his father Howard and his teacher Benjamin Graham. Ben Graham's philosophy had such an impact on Buffett that he enrolled in Columbia Business School to study directly under him. Later, Buffett's claimed: "I'm 15 percent Fisher and 85 percent Benjamin Graham."

Charles Thomas Munger was born on January 1, 1924, in Omaha, Nebraska. He is Vice-Chairman of Berkshire Hathaway Corporation and Chairman of Wesco Financial Corporation. After studies at the University of Michigan and service in the U.S. Navy, he entered Harvard Law School. In 1948, he founded and worked as a real estate attorney at Munger, Tolles & Olson LLP until 1965. Munger's hero is Benjamin Franklin. Munger talks about the concept of "Elementary, Worldly Wisdom" as it relates to business and finance. This consists of a set of mental models framed as a latticework that can help one solve a critical business problem. Munger ran a successful investment partnership of his own from 1962 to 1975. According to Buffett's essay, "The Superinvestors of Graham and Doddsville", Munger's investment partnership generated compound annual returns of 19.8% during the 1962-75 period compared to a 5.0% annual appreciation rate for the Dow.

Buffett and Munger met in 1959. Munger had moved to southern California, but he returned to Omaha for a visit when his father died. Dr. Davis brought them together at a dinner in a local Omaha restaurant. Munger's investment partnership in Los Angeles, and Buffett's in Omaha, were similar in approach; both sought to purchase some discount to underlying value. They both outperformed the Dow Jones Industrial Average by impressive margins. They also transformed Berkshire Hathaway from a textile manufacturer into a successful investment holding company. Their long-term economic goal at Berkshire Hathaway is to maximize the average annual rate of gain in intrinsic business value on a per-share basis. They do not measure the economic significance or performance of Berkshire by its size. They measure it by per-share progress.

We believe that our formula - the purchase at sensible prices of businesses that have good underlying economics and are run by honest and able people - is certain to produce reasonable success. We expect, therefore, to keep on doing well. Warren Buffett[13]

"You need a different checklist and different mental models for different companies. I can never make it easy by saying, 'Here are three things.' You have to derive it yourself to ingrain it in your head for the rest of your life." Charlie Munger[14]

MY FRAME OF REFERENCE

In the development of our understanding, how should we frame an investment idea? In my quest, I look to the best for answers. In developing an understanding of a business and its products, Warren Buffett framed the careful mental process this way: "If I were looking at a company, I would put myself in the frame of mind that I had just inherited that company, and it was the only asset my family was ever going to own. What would I do with it? What am I thinking about? What am I worried about? Who are my customers? Go out and talk to them. Find out the strengths and weaknesses of this particular company versus other ones."[15]

This is the behavioral process of elaboration. It is the bit of mental work that helps us frame and earn a clearer mental picture of reality. According to the Merriam-Webster dictionary, elaboration means "to work out in detail." Do your elaboration carefully, and you will be better prepared to see genuine opportunity. Like a detective trying to develop an understanding of a case, Buffett begins by asking himself basic questions. Warren Buffett and Charlie Munger look for simple things they can count and able managers they can trust. They look for businesses run by able and owner-oriented people.

Play with the four filter criteria and twist them into 4 behavioral business clusters this way: 1. Products 2. Customers 3. Management 4. Margin of Safety. After many hours of thought and play, I concluded that the Four Filters are a remarkable intellectual achievement. The Four Filters algorithm effectively combines the use of both qualitative and quantitative factors. The filters encapsulate the most important elements of business endurance and investing profitability. Using inversion to find 1 out of 1,000, the Four Filters help us eliminate the lesser 999.

As we progress, how do we develop a better frame of reference? How should we make better investing decisions? How do we increase the probability of success and minimize the probability of failure. How do we reduce our risks and maximize our earnings?

I became interested in better understanding how Buffett and Munger frame their decisions during business school at Purdue University Calumet. Thanks to Roger Lowenstein for writing the 1995 biography, "Buffett: The Making of an American

Capitalist."[16] This was the book that first captured my interest in Mr. Buffett, value investing, and efficient business thought. In addition to the writings of Warren Buffett and Charlie Munger, I have also enjoyed reading the fine books written by Benjamin Graham, Philip Fisher, Philip Carret, Andy Kilpatrick, Janet Lowe, Warren Boroson, Robert Hagstrom, Robert Miles, Bruce Greenwald, Timothy Vick, Michelle Leder, Christopher Browne, and Charles Mizrahi.

My deep interest in "decision making" has been focused on the Behavioral Finance area I call "successful practitioner framing." Framing in behavioral finance is the choosing of particular words to present a given set of facts. And, framing can influence our choices. Tversky and Kahneman described "Prospect Theory" in 1979 using framed questions.[17] They found that contrary to expected utility theory, people placed different weights on gains and losses. Tversky and Kahneman found that individuals are much more distressed by prospective losses than they are happy by equivalent gains. Some have concluded that investors typically consider the loss of $1 twice as painful as the pleasure received from a $1 gain. Others believe this work helps to explain patterns of irrationality, inconsistency, and incompetence in the ways human beings arrive at decisions and choices when faced with uncertainty. An increasing body of literature on framing supports a tendency for people to take more risks when seeking to avoid losses as opposed to securing gains. In 1992, Takemura[18] showed that the effects of framing are likely to be lower when subjects are warned in advance that they will be required to justify their choices, and when more time is allowed for arriving at their choices. Luckily, Buffett and Munger seem to have arrived at the practical use of these optimal framing ideas earlier than most. They make good use of "justification," "elaboration," "elimination," "probability," and "time."

In trying to understand a business, remember that Warren Buffett frames his mental approach in an elaborative way. He imagines he has just inherited a company, and it was the only asset his family was ever going to own. What would he need to know about this company if it were the only thing he could own for the rest of his life?[19] This illustrates that Buffett practices a rational framing of companies and their products. In business school they call it SWOT analysis; looking for the Strengths, Weaknesses, Opportunities, and Threats to a business. So, how do Buffett and Munger frame their investment decisions? They use the Four Filters this way: "We look for understandable first-class businesses, with enduring competitive advantages, accompanied

our understanding. Munger also advises students to learn from the "instructive dead;" to learn from wise heroes who have passed on a legacy of useful wisdom.[23] Using our acquired knowledge, and applying rational valuation steps will help enhance our understanding of a business and its products. Qualitative valuation is very important. Investors will take different approaches to measuring both quantitative and qualitative values. Charlie Munger says "We all are learning, modifying, or destroying ideas all the time." Munger believes that the rapid destruction of our ideas when the time is right is one of the most valuable qualities we can acquire. He urges students to force themselves to consider arguments on the other side – inversion.[24]

Why should we use checklists? There is one hint found in a a portion of a speech called The Psychology of Human Misjudgment by Charles T. Munger. My example here is Charlie Munger's Error #18. The Availability-Misweighing Tendency. Charlie Munger says that "the brain can't use what it can't remember or what it is blocked from recognizing because it is heavily influenced by one or more psychological tendencies bearing strongly on it." So the mind overweighs what is easily available and thus displays what he calls an Availability-Misweighing Tendency. Charlie says that an idea is not worth more merely because it is easily available. He said "the main antidotes to miscues from Availability-Misweighing Tendency often involve procedures, including use of checklists, which are almost always helpful. Another antidote is to behave somewhat like Darwin did when he emphasized disconfirming evidence." Charlie Munger favors taking a skeptical approach like Darwin, and looking at the notions that are opposite to the incumbent notions.

The Four Filters Investing Formula delivers something valuable. The Four Filters serve as a set of "Investing Best Practices." They help us develop better "self-control." The Four Filters help us avoid costly mistakes and they motivate us to focus on "Wonderful Businesses." And, the Four Filters promote investing "self-discipline." Best of all, the Four Filters help get us closer to understanding the "nature" and "intrinsic value" of a good business investment prospect. With practice, we can learn to use the four filters more effectively. However, if we do not understand a business and its products well, Warren Buffett and Charlie Munger advise inactivity.[25]

An excerpt on realism, circle of competence, simplicity, and avoiding mistakes.

"What counts for most people in investing is not how much they know, but rather how realistically they define what they don't know. An investor needs to do very few things right as long as he or she avoids big mistakes... "Keep it simple. If you are right about a business whose value is largely dependent on a single key factor that is both easy to understand and enduring, the payoff is the same as if you had correctly analyzed an investment alternative characterized by constantly shifting and complex variables. We try to price, rather than time, purchases." Warren Buffett[26]

CHAPTER ONE OF FIVE: UNDERSTANDING

Filter Number One:

Develop an Understanding of a Business and its Products.

My goal in this chapter is to review a bit of history, mention a few concepts, and stimulate a growth in your latticework of understanding businesses and situations. Since this is a short book, it will not teach you everything you need to know. However, these bits and pieces may add up in your mind to help you become a better investor. This chapter displays a wider landscape made up of smaller pictures from some of Warren Buffett's Partnerships and Berkshire Hathaway's historical investment examples. This way, readers can refer to the books listed in the endnotes for greater details. There are many great books and additional resources listed at the end of this book. And, our understanding develops each time we add samples or building blocks to our mental models of reality, perceptions, and misperceptions. Warren Buffett puts it this way: "Seek whatever information will further your understanding of a company's business."[27] On the other hand, Charlie Munger likes to say: "We just throw some decisions into the 'too hard' file and go onto others."[28] So, like beauty, understanding resides in the mind of the beholder.

In developing our deeper understanding of a business, read, study, look, listen, think, visualize, feel emotions, calculate profit, and learn. Charlie Munger brings a keen critical mind to the game. He advises us to build an understanding like a "latticework of mental models" based on facts with accurate and reality based impressions.[29] Look for popular consumer brands and potential "upward" pricing power. Also, keep in mind that understanding a business and its products is a cumulative process. Thinking more about filter #2: "Sustainable Competitive Advantage," and filter #3: "Able and Trustworthy Managers" will build a more solid base to your foundation of understanding a business.

For a quick start to understanding a business, take a look at a company's Free Cash Flow to the Firm, (FCFF). It is the amount of cash left over after the payment of the investments and taxes. (FCFF = NOP – Taxes – Net Investment – Net Change in Working Capital). If FCFF is solid, then the business is serving customers and is making a profit. A business generates revenue by selling its products and services. In generating revenue, a business incurs expenses—salaries, cost of goods sold (CGS), selling and general administrative expenses (SGA), research and development (R&D). The difference between operating revenue and operating expense is Operating Income or Net Operating Profit. The key figures for us to focus upon are the numbers seen after all the costs are accounted for.

For a quick start to eliminating "suspect companies," or ones we want to avoid, look for bad terminology. In 2002, Buffett wrote "bad terminology is the enemy of good thinking." He warned us that companies or investment professionals using terms such as "EBITDA" and "pro forma," want us to unthinkingly accept concepts that are dangerously flawed. Charlie Munger has called EBITDA (Earnings Before Interest Taxes Depreciation and Amortization), "Bullshit Earnings."[30]

Example number one worth understanding is a simple section from the 1960 Buffett Partnership Letter. It illustrates the quick recognition of additional business value. This excerpt illustrates Warren Buffett's keen understanding of a single business's unique and valuable situation:

"Last year (1959) I mentioned a new commitment (Sanborn Map Co.) which involved about 25% of the assets of the various partnerships. Presently (1960), this investment is about 35% of assets. This is an unusually large percentage, but has been made for strong reasons. In effect, this company is partially an investment trust owning some thirty or forty other securities of high quality. Our investment was made and is carried at a substantial discount from asset value based on market value of their securities and a conservative appraisal of the operating business... For seventy-five years the business operated in a more or less monopolistic manner with profits realized in every year accompanied by almost complete immunity to recession and lack of need for any sales effort... There were no capital requirements to the business so that any retained earnings could be devoted to this project. Over a period of time about $2.5 million was invested, roughly half in bonds and half in stocks. Thus, in the last decade particularly, the investment portfolio blossomed while the operating map business wilted."[31]

Example number two shows us that the development of Buffett's and Munger's understanding of business is very much intertwined with their GEICO experience. GEICO is presented as an example because I believe it had a big impact in Warren Buffett's understanding of other businesses in general. For Buffett and Munger, their oversight of the 1976-1980 GEICO turnaround was an important learning experience for two basic reasons. First, they were impressed by the "managerial brilliance" of Jack Byrne. Secondly, they found that the fundamental business advantage GEICO had enjoyed was still intact. Although GEICO was still submerged in a sea of financial and operating troubles, GEICO was designed to be the low-cost operation in the marketplace of auto insurance.[32] And, the 1984 letter shows Buffett using the term "sustainable competitive advantage" in relation to GEICO. Warren Buffett reported to shareholders of Berkshire: "You have benefited in enormous measure from the talents of GEICO's Jack Byrne, Bill Snyder, and Lou Simpson. In its core business (low-cost auto and homeowners insurance), GEICO has a major, sustainable competitive advantage. That is a rare asset in business generally, and it's almost non-existent in the field of financial services."[33]

Sometimes, as much as we would like, we cannot hurry an education. GEICO is an example illustrating the multi year exposure and education for Warren Buffett that goes back to 1951. In December of that year, Lorimer "Davy" Davidson spent four hours explaining the merits of GEICO to business student Warren Buffett. Buffett believes that "no one has ever received a better half-day course in how the insurance industry functions nor in the factors that enable one company to excel over others."[34] However, temptation struck him in 1952, and Buffett sold his entire GEICO position for $15,259, primarily to buy into Western Insurance Securities. Western was selling for slightly more than one times its earnings, a p/e ratio that caught his attention.[35]

Robert Hagstrom, in his book, "The Warren Buffett Way," made an interesting observation. He wrote: "Warren Buffett understands the insurance business in a way that few others do. His success derives in large part from acknowledging the essential commodity nature of the industry and elevating his insurance companies to the level of a franchise."[36]

In the development of his understanding, keep in mind that Warren Buffett's biggest advantage is passion and attitude for sensible investing. He brings an intensity to the game. He learned from Ben Graham that the key to successful investing was the purchase of shares in good businesses when market prices were at a large discount from underlying business values. The gradual movement towards buying high quality "first-class businesses" was an important boost in the right direction. Sound owner-oriented business principles, along with time, training, temperament, and experience have made Buffett and Munger even better investors. Said Buffett, "Our criteria have nothing to do with maximizing immediately reportable earnings; our goal, rather, is to maximize eventual net worth."[37] This means maximizing intrinsic value per share.

Examples three and four are the Coca-Cola and Gillette investments. Both have strong brand loyalty and solid cost of production controls. Warren Buffett said in 1993 "the might of their brand names, the attributes of their products, and the strength of their distribution systems give them an enormous competitive advantage, setting up a protective moat around their economic castles. The average company, in contrast, does battle daily without any such means of protection."[38] In 2005 Gillette was bought by Proctor and Gamble, and it continues to be a strong competitor.

Now, let's back up even further in order to understand the bigger investing picture. Considered the Dean of Investment Analysis, Ben Graham also added much to the development of the first of Four Filters, "Understanding." Perhaps many of you thought

Graham was just about buying cheap bargains. If that were true, he would not have been called the "Father of Security Analysis." According to Buffett, Ben Graham (former Chairman of GEICO) added three basic ideas that can enhance our investing framework.[39] Graham's ideas can help us do reasonably well in stocks. According to Warren Buffett, Graham's three basic ideas are:

1. We should look at stocks as part ownership of a business,
2. We should look at market fluctuations in terms of his "Mr. Market" example and make them our friend rather than our enemy. We can learn to profit from market folly rather than participate in it.
3. The three most important words in investing are "Margin of Safety."

Ben Graham talked about safety in his last chapter of *The Intelligent Investor*. And, notice that it is the pivotal fourth and final determining step, of the Four Filters evaluation process. The Four Filters are an intellectual advancement encapsulating Graham's three fundamental ideas. These ideas have been enhanced further by adding investigation into "enduring competitive advantage"[40] and "able and trustworthy managers."[41]

By now, you may be wondering how rehashing history can help you better understand a single business. Allow me to explain. In developing our understanding of a business and its products, the Four Filters force us to think for ourselves. All four clusters of thought and understanding are important for long-term investing success. Like Buffett, we can read annual reports of a company we are interested in. Then, we can read the annual reports of the competitors. In order to build a better framework of understanding, we can collect mental facts about businesses like some people collect baseball cards. Mr. Buffett has said annual reports are the main source of the study material needed for understanding.[42]

Look for strengths, weaknesses, opportunities, threats, successes, errors, and failures. Warren Buffett says "Charlie likes to study errors and I have generated ample material for him in our textile and insurance businesses."[43] Warren Buffett cautions students to focus on their own circle of competence. Notice the filtering process within his statement here: "Draw a circle around the businesses you understand and then eliminate those that fail to qualify on the basis of value, good management, and limited exposure to hard times."[44] A big part of his evaluation process is to cast out businesses that are too difficult to understand. We can focus on "easy to understand businesses" with good returns on equity. We should begin to build up a mental checklist of factors we like and dislike about a business. Where did Munger and Buffett's checklist influences come from? Phil Carret and Philip Fisher both developed and used quality checklists.[45] Carret's and Fisher's criteria are illustrated in a table at the end of this chapter. There you can also find Charlie Munger's list of human behavioral tendencies.[46]

Warren Buffett understands that "the best business to own is one that over an extended period can employ large amounts of incremental capital at very high rates of return. The worst business to own is one that must, or will, consistently employ ever-greater amounts of capital at very low rates of return. Unfortunately, the first type of business is very hard to find: Most high-return businesses need relatively little capital. Shareholders of such a business usually will benefit if it pays out most of its earnings in dividends or makes significant stock repurchases."[47]

Just as a good leader has been tested by tough times and has a solid followership, high-return investors should remember that a good business will have a loyal followership or customer base. The wonderful ones will have some additional sort of pricing power. Adding a powerful driver to this process, Charlie Munger understood the importance of thinking about the "Wonderful Business" early, while Warren Buffett was still buying cheap "Cigar-Butts."[48]   Shortly after purchasing Berkshire, Buffett acquired a Baltimore department store called Hochschild Kohn. It was purchased through a retailing company called Diversified Retailing that later merged with Berkshire Hathaway. They now consider this, as well as the original textile business purchase, an investing mistake.   They were investing mistakes because they were businesses that did not have enduring competitive advantages.   Therefore, they were destined for rough competition and diminishing profits.   We will make investing mistakes. However, we must learn from our mistakes. We must learn to limit our losses and maximize our gains. We should also strive to learn from the "**best practices**" of the best practitioners of investing.

Both Buffett and Munger admit they have learned from their mistakes. And, they have learned how to seek businesses with better economic prospects. Now, when buying companies or common stocks, they look for first-class businesses accompanied by first-class managements. Charles Mizrahi, friend and author of Getting Started in Value Investing" likes to say: "They look to what managements do, more than what managements say."[49]

Warren Buffett learned valuable ideas from studying Phil Fisher, Philip Carret, and Henry Singleton. Buffett met Phil Fisher in the early Sixties, after reading his first book. Phil Fisher was a deep thinker into the nature of managements and their business growth potential. Some of Fisher's ideas are included later in chapter three. According to Warren Buffett, "His ideas, like those of Ben Graham, were simple but powerful", and Buffett wanted to meet the man whose teachings had such an influence on him.[50] So, we can see that part of developing our "circle of competence" is reading, learning, observing and integrating sound ideas into our investment philosophy. Buffett and Munger read the newspapers, think about a few of the big propositions, and go by their own sense of probabilities.[51] Buffett and Munger's long-term economic goal at Berkshire Hathaway is to maximize the average annual rate of gain in intrinsic business value on a per-share basis.[52] Conceptualizing "Intrinsic business value on a per-share basis" should be learned by every good investor and every good earnings manager.

As shareholders, we want to see free cash flow. We want to see retained earnings continue to grow annually. This may fluctuate from year to year, but the general trend should be upward. We can have faith in the managements of businesses who utilize retained earnings effectively; and translate a dollar retained into a dollar or more of subsequent market value for us.

You will develop a better understanding of a business, its products, and its managers if you can measure it building intrinsic business value on a per-share basis. And, if well-run companies have opportunities to employ additional capital advantageously, retained earnings can build a value to shareholders greater than 100 cents on the dollar.

We can learn to better understand a business and its competitors by using and integrating all these tools in a sensible and logical way. A study of financial history is also useful for building our knowledge base about businesses and the economic times they compete in. I like "The New York Times Century of Business" by Floyd Norris and Christine Bockelmann.[53] It describes historical business events including the 1901 "Northern Pacific Corner."

On May 3, 1901, Edward Harriman devised a plan to buy a controlling interest in the Northern Pacific Railroad and use its power on the Burlington to place friendly directors on the board. Since an excess of shares were bought on margin with excessive speculative zeal, the Harriman-Hill entanglement created stock price chaos and panic on the stock market. Harriman's stock raid became known as the Northern Pacific Corner. Three days later, Harriman and James Hill had to work to settle the chaos for brokers in order to avoid a wider stock market panic.

In addition, studying the next three filters will add to your "latticework of understanding" the nature of a business. Munger said, "To understand a business, figure out what results it is achieving, why it is getting those results, and what could happen to change what is causing those results." Buffett and Munger are aware that we can easily fool ourselves. Therefore, they practice these mental checklist mechanisms to minimize the possibility of foolish errors.

In a 2002 talk about investing, Charlie Munger described the self-development process this way: "If you're going to be an investor, you're going to make some investments where you don't have all the experience you need. But if you keep trying to get a little better over time, you'll start to make investments that are virtually certain to have a good outcome. The keys are discipline, hard work, and practice. It's like playing golf -- you have to work on it."

Charlie Munger and Warren Buffett insist on spending quiet time to just sit and think. Charlie Munger said: "That is very uncommon in American business. We read and think. So Warren and I do more reading and thinking and less doing than most people in business. We do that because we like that kind of a life."[54]

From The Psychology of Human Misjudgment by Charles T. Munger, Error #19 is called the "Use-It-or-Lose-It Tendency."[55]

"All skills attenuate with disuse. I was a whiz at calculus until age twenty, after which the skill was soon obliterated by total nonuse. The right antidote to such a loss is to make use of the functional equivalent of the aircraft simulator employed in pilot training. This allows a pilot to continuously practice all of the rarely used skills that he can't afford to lose.

Throughout his life, a wise man engages in practice of all his useful, rarely used skills, many of them outside his discipline, as a sort of duty to his better self. If he reduces the number of skills he practices and, therefore, the number of skills he retains, he will naturally drift into error from man with a hammer tendency. His learning capacity will also shrink as he creates gaps in the latticework of theory he needs as a framework for

---

understanding new experience. It is also essential for a thinking man to assemble his skills into a checklist that he routinely uses. Any other mode of operation will cause him to miss much that is important."

An Investing Principles Checklist From Poor Charlie's Almanack:[56]
(http://valueinvestingworld.blogspot.com/2007/12/investing-principles-checklist-from.html)

1. Risk – All investment evaluations should begin by measuring risk, especially reputational
Incorporate an appropriate margin of safety
Avoid dealing with people of questionable character
Insist upon proper compensation for risk assumed
Always beware of inflation and interest rate exposures
Avoid big mistakes; shun permanent capital loss

2. Independence – "Only in fairy tales are emperors told they are naked"
Objectivity and rationality require independence of thought
Remember that just because other people agree or disagree with you doesn't make you right or wrong – the only thing that matters is the correctness of your analysis and judgment. Mimicking the herd invites regression to the mean (merely average performance)

3. Preparation – "The only way to win is to work, work, work, work, and hope to have a few insights"
Develop into a lifelong self-learner through voracious reading; cultivate curiosity and strive to become a little wiser every day

More important than the will to win is the will to prepare

Develop fluency in mental models from the major academic disciplines

If you want to get smart, the question you have to keep asking is "why, why, why?"

4. Intellectual humility – Acknowledging what you don't know is the dawning of wisdom

Stay within a well-defined circle of competence

Identify and reconcile disconfirming evidence

Resist the craving for false precision, false certainties, etc.

Above all, never fool yourself, and remember that you are the easiest person to fool

"Understanding both the power of compound interest and the difficulty of getting it is the heart and soul of understanding a lot of things."

5. Analytic rigor – Use of the scientific method and effective checklists minimizes errors and omissions

Determine value apart from price; progress apart from activity; wealth apart from size

It is better to remember the obvious than to grasp the esoteric

Be a business analyst, not a market, macroeconomic, or security analyst

Consider totality of risk and effect; look always at potential second order and higher level impacts

Think forwards and backwards – Invert, always invert

6. Allocation – Proper allocation of capital is an investor's number one job

Remember that highest and best use is always measured by the next best use (opportunity cost)

Good ideas are rare – when the odds are greatly in your favor, bet (allocate) heavily

Don't "fall in love" with an investment – be situation-dependent and opportunity-driven

7. Patience – Resist the natural human bias to act

"Compound interest is the eighth wonder of the world" (Einstein); never interrupt it unnecessarily

Avoid unnecessary transactional taxes and frictional costs; never take action for its own sake

Be alert for the arrival of luck

Enjoy the process along with the proceeds, because the process is where you live

8. Decisiveness – When proper circumstances present themselves, act with decisiveness and conviction

Be fearful when others are greedy, and greedy when others are fearful

Opportunity doesn't come often, so seize it when it comes

Opportunity meeting the prepared mind; that's the game

9. Change – Live with change and accept unremovable complexity

Recognize and adapt to the true nature of the world around you; don't expect it to adapt to you

Continually challenge and willingly amend your "best-loved ideas"

Recognize reality even when you don't like it – especially when you don't like it

10. Focus – Keep things simple and remember what you set out to do

Remember that reputation and integrity are your most valuable assets – and can be lost in a heartbeat

Guard against the effects of hubris (arrogance) and boredom

Don't overlook the obvious by drowning in minutiae (the small details)

Be careful to exclude unneeded information or slop: "A small leak can sink a great ship"

Face your big troubles; don't sweep them under the rug.

Charlie Munger's list of psychology-based tendencies. Charlie says that, while these tendencies are generally useful, they can often mislead. So, being aware of these human tendencies can help us think more rationally when we attempt to understand things.

1.   Reward and Punishment Superresponse Tendency

2.   Liking/Loving Tendency

3.   Disliking/Hating Tendency

4.   Doubt-Avoidance Tendency

5.   Inconsistency-Avoidance Tendency

6.   Curiosity Tendency

7.   Kantian Fairness Tendency

8.   Envy/Jealousy Tendency

9.   Reciprocation Tendency

10.   Influence-from-Mere Association Tendency

11.   Simple, Pain-Avoiding Psychological Denial

12.   Excessive Self-Regard Tendency

13.   Overoptimism Tendency

14.   Deprival Superreaction Tendency

15.   Social-Proof Tendency

16.   Contrast-Misreaction Tendency

17.   Stress-Influence Tendency

18.   Availability-Misweighing Tendency

19.   Use-It-or-Lose-It Tendency

20.   Drug-Misinfluence Tendency

21.   Senescence-Misinfluence Tendency

22.   Authority-Misinfluence Tendency

23.   Twaddle Tendency

24.   Reason-Respecting Tendency

25.   Lollapalooza Tendency – The Tendency to Get Extreme Confluences of Psychological Tendencies Acting in Favor of a Particular Outcome.

Warren Buffett on Phil Fisher[57]

"When I met him, I was as impressed by the man as by his ideas. Much like Ben Graham, Fisher was unassuming, generous in spirit and an extraordinary teacher. From him I learned the value of the "scuttlebutt' approach: Go out and talk to competitors, suppliers, customers to find out how an industry or a company really operates. A thorough understanding of the business, obtained by using Phil's techniques, combined with the quantitative discipline taught by Ben, will enable one to make intelligent investment commitments. I am an eager reader of whatever Phil has to say, and I recommend him to you."

Charlie Munger on Phil Fisher[58]

"I always like it when someone attractive to me agrees with me, so I have fond memories of Phil Fisher. The idea that it was hard to find good investments, so concentrate in a few, seems to me to be an obviously good idea."

Warren Buffett on Phil Carret[59]

"Phil's a hero of mine. He had the best long term investment record of anyone I know". Carret's success was recognition of the value of certain small dull companies before other experts were aware of them. He did not mind sitting dead in the water for long periods. He was a friends of both Howard Buffett, and son, Warren Buffett. He wrote a series of articles for Barron's which were published in book form as The Art of Speculation. Investing referred to buying bonds in those days. If it were issued today, the book would probably called The Art of Investing.

Phil Carret on Management from Warren Boroson's book.[60]

Q. In evaluating a company, how important is management?

P.C. Management is the important factor in a company. Anyone who gets to be chairman or president of a company is a fairly smooth operator, and talks a good fight, you know. You have to look at his record—how much of his own money is in the stock (my yardstick is a year's salary)—and is he wildly optimistic or cautious? If he says things are pretty good and the results were very good, that's great. If he says things are fine and there's a lousy quarter, I don't want his stock.

"Phil Carret was one of the most towering intellects I have ever known. He had an amazing analytical mind and was extremely perceptive and forward looking, all tempered with a gracious and gentle sense of humor. He disdained arrogance and sarcasm." Frank Betz, Carret/Zane Capital Management[61]

Carret's "12 Commandments of Investing":

1. Never hold fewer than 10 different securities covering five different fields of business;
2. At least once every six months, reappraise every security held;
3. Keep at least half the total fund in income producing securities;
4. Consider yield the least important factor in analyzing any stock;
5. Be quick to take losses and reluctant to take profits;
6. Never put more than 25% of a given fund into securities about which detailed information is not readily and regularly available;
7. Avoid inside information as you would the plague;
8. Seek facts diligently, advice never;
9. Ignore mechanical formulas for value in securities;
10. When stocks are high, money rates rising and business prosperous, at least half a given fund should be placed in short-term bonds;
11. Borrow money sparingly and only when stocks are low, money rates low and falling and business depressed;
12. Set aside a moderate proportion of available funds for the purchase of long-term options on stocks in promising companies whenever available.

Phillip Fisher's 15 Questions Checklist:

1.Does the company have products or services with sufficient market potential to make possible a sizable increase in sales for at least several years?

2.Does the management have a determination to continue to develop products or processes that will further increase total sales potentials when the growth potentials of currently attractive product lines have largely been exploited?

3.How effective are the company's research and development efforts in relation to its size?

4.Does the company have an above-average sales organization?

5.Does the company have a worthwhile profit margin?

6.What is the company doing to maintain or improve profit margins?

7.Does the company have outstanding labor and personnel relations?

8.Does the company have outstanding executive relations?

9.Does the company have depth to its management?

10.How good are the company's cost analysis and accounting controls?

11.Are there other aspects of the business, somewhat peculiar to the industry involved, which will give the investor important clues as to how outstanding the company may be in relation to its competition?

12.Does the company have a short-range or long-range outlook in regard to profits?

13.In the foreseeable future will the growth of the company require sufficient equity financing so that the larger number of shares then outstanding will largely cancel the existing stockholder's benefit from this anticipated growth?

14.Does the management talk freely to investors about its affairs when things are going well but "clam up" when troubles and disappointments occur?

15.Does the company have a management of unquestionable integrity?

CHAPTER TWO OF FIVE:
SUSTAINABLE COMPETITIVE ADVANTAGE

Filter Number Two:

Does a Business have a Sustainable Competitive Advantage?

Since the nature of Capitalism is Competition, a successful business needs to have "something special" in order to lead the pack and fend off competitors. The two major types of competitive advantage are 1. a cost advantage, and 2. a differentiation advantage.[62] Our quest to find such businesses requires us to ask a lot of questions. What is the nature of the business over the next twenty years? Can we predict it with a high degree of accuracy? Can we imagine an enduring competitive advantage? Is there something special here? Is this advantage eroding? Are we being rational and realistic about our assessment?

Benjamin Graham urged his students to analyze the business. Sustainable Competitive Advantage is also called "favorable long-term prospects" or "enduring economic advantages." Sustainable Competitive Advantage comes from things that make a business difficult to copy. It is a barrier to entry that endures. A protected brand is such a barrier because it represents something unique and valued in the mind of a customer. A valuable patent or trademark can give a firm a period of protected advantage, acting as a barrier to entry.

In investing, the common intellectual advantage of the investors from Graham-and-Doddsville is also their competitive advantage. Their search for a "Margin of Safety" is their advantage. The Superinvestors of Graham-and-Doddsville seem to do a better job in looking and finding discrepancies between the value of a business and the price of small pieces of that business in the market.[63] Finding quality bargains is their profitable "variant perception."[64] Warren Buffett and Charlie Munger added to this foundation of bargain hunting by looking for a business with a big protective moat around it. Buffett and Munger look for "Something special in peoples' minds." "Brands" "Technology" "Patent Protection" "Location" "Cost of Production" "Distribution System" "Local Service."[65]

At Stanford, one of Fisher's business classes had required him to accompany his professor on periodic visits to companies in the San Francisco area. The professor would get the business managers to talk about their operations, and often helped them solve an immediate problem. Driving back to Stanford, Fisher and his professor would recap what they observed about the companies and managers they visited. "That hour each week," Fisher said, "was the most useful training I ever received."5 …From these experiences, Fisher came to believe that people could make superior profits by (1) investing in companies with above-average potential and (2) aligning themselves with the most capable management. To isolate these exceptional companies, Fisher developed a point system that qualified a company by the characteristics of its business and its management.

So what makes one business thrive better than another business? Look for the protective "Moat" around a business's economic castle. Is it enduring or sustainable?

Charlie Munger recommended the autobiography of Les Schwab "Les Schwab Pride in Performance: Keep It Going," at the 2004

Berkshire Hathaway annual meeting. According to Munger, "Schwab ran tire shops in the Midwest and made a fortune by being shrewd in a tough business by having good systems."

The cost advantage present at GEICO insurance is a barrier for competitors. Can they match GEICO in cost or service? According to Buffett, GEICO's direct marketing gave it an enormous cost advantage over competitors that sold through agents. And what about size and capital rating?[67] Well, GEICO certainly has strong backing. And, Berkshire Hathaway's other insurance and reinsurance operations also benefit from the size, rating, and "time tested" soundness of its capital base.

One of my favorite Buffett quotes reminds me of "time travel", and it goes like this: "Time is the friend of the wonderful business, the enemy of the mediocre. You might think this principle is obvious, but I had to learn it the hard way. In fact, I had to learn it several times over."[68] This ability to endure over time, in good times and in bad, and continue to earn a solid profit is an important competitive advantage. And, sometimes, that comes about because of decent economics plus superior managements who work to build an even stronger moat. So, the

"Wonderful Business"[69] will certainly include a strong, protective and lasting moat.

Talking about less competitive and weaker businesses, Warren Buffett said: "In many industries, differentiation simply can't be made meaningful. A few producers in such industries may consistently do well if they have a cost advantage that is both wide and sustainable." However, these are a few exceptional businesses. In many industries, such enduring winners do not exist. So, for the great majority of businesses selling "commodity" products, Buffett believes that a depressing equation of business economics prevails. In his words, "a persistent over-capacity without administered prices (or costs) equals poor profitability."[70]

Buffett and Munger like strong brands like Coke and Gillette and Kraft. These companies have increased their worldwide shares of market in recent years. Their brand names, the attributes of their products, and the strength of their distribution systems give them competitive advantage. The average company, in contrast, does not have such protection.[71]

So what does this sustainable competitive advantage look like in numbers? Take a look at Chapter Six of Charles Mizrahi's book "Getting Started in Value Investing." It has a good section where Mizrahi discusses ROE (Return on Equity) and NPM (Net Profit Margin).[72] Next, consider why the Coca-Cola Company is such a good business from an investor's point of view. Both Coke and Pepsi make products we enjoy. As an investor, I prefer the Coca-Cola Company. One reason is the amount of Free Cash Flow generated for every sale. Another reason is the amount of Free Cash Flow generated after expenses. Take a look at this chart from Morningstar:[73]

Coca-Cola Company (KO)	1998	1999	2000	2001	2002	2003	2004	2005	2006	2007	TTM
Free Cash Flow/Sales	13.66%	14.21%	13.94%	16.63%	19.89%	22.07%	23.74%	23.91%	18.89%	19.07%	19.07%
Free Cash Flow/Net Income	0.73	1.16	1.31	0.84	1.28	1.07	1.07 1.08	1.13	0.9	0.92	91.99
PepsiCo, Inc. (PEP)	1998	1999	2000	2001	2002	2003	2004	2005	2006	2007	TTM
Free Cash Flow/Sales	8.08%	9.37%	13.92%	10.68%	12.70%	11.06%	12.53%	12.64%	11.43%	11.41%	11.41%
Free Cash Flow/Net Income	0.91	0.93	1.30	1.08	0.96	0.84	0.87	1.01	0.71	0.80	79.60

If you were unaware of the concept of "free cash generating efficiency" prior to now, then perhaps you are beginning to like my book. Yes, I too was "innocent" and ignorant to these facts prior to studying Buffett and Munger.

In 1991, I was running a high-overhead business in a competitive marketplace. That year, Buffett commented on the competitive arena of insurance. He said, "Insurers will always need huge amounts of reinsurance protection for marine and aviation disasters as well as for natural catastrophes. In the 1980's much of this reinsurance was supplied by "innocents" - that is, by insurers that did not understand the risks of the business - but they have now been financially burned beyond recognition." (Berkshire itself was an innocent all too often when I was personally running the insurance operation.) Insurers, though, like investors, eventually repeat their mistakes."[74] As for me, I do not wish to repeat my innocent mistakes.

Thanks to Roger Lowenstein and his 1995 book, "Buffett: The Making of an American Capitalist," I started to learn about Buffett, Munger, Graham, and many others in the world of value investing.[75] In the world of marketing super-catastrophe insurance, Buffett said Berkshire Hathaway will enjoy a significant competitive advantage because of its premier financial strength.[76]

In the 2001 Letter to Shareholders, there is an excerpt about NetJets scale advantage. "Both we and our customers derive significant operational benefits from our being the runaway leader in the fractional ownership business… The ubiquity of our fleet also reduces our "positioning" costs below those incurred by operators with smaller fleets. These advantages of scale, and others we have, give NetJets a significant economic edge over competition."[77]   In another Berkshire Hathaway business, the Borsheims jewelry subsidiary attracts business nationwide because of having several advantages that competitors can't match. Warren Buffett wrote that "the most important item in the equation is our operating costs, which run about 18% of sales compared to 40% or so at the typical competitor. (Included in the 18% are occupancy and buying costs, which some public companies include in "cost of goods sold.") Just as Wal-Mart, with its 15% operating costs, sells at prices that high-cost competitors can't touch and thereby constantly increases its market share, so does Borsheim's. What works with diapers works with diamonds.[78] Our low prices create huge volume that in turn allows us to carry an extraordinarily broad inventory of goods, running ten or more times the size of that at the typical fine-jewelry store. Couple our breadth of selection and low prices with superb service and you can understand how Ike and his family have built a national jewelry phenomenon from an Omaha location."

Interestingly, in the 1989 Letter, Buffett said "NFM and Borsheim's follow precisely the same formula for success: (1) unparalleled depth and breadth of merchandise at one location; (2) the lowest operating costs in the business; (3) the shrewdest of buying, made possible in part by the huge volumes purchased; (4) gross margins, and therefore prices, far below competitors'; and (5) friendly personalized service with family members on hand at all times."

How does practical competitive advantage tie in with current academic thought? In his book, "Competition Demystified", Bruce Greenwald of Columbia University presented a new and simplified approach to business strategy.[79] The conventional approach to strategy taught in business schools is based on Michael Porter's work. In Porter's model it is easy for students to get lost in a sophisticated model of your competitors, suppliers, buyers, substitutes, and other players.[80] Greenwald warns us to not lose sight of the big question: "Are there barriers to entry that allow us to do things that other firms cannot?" Then, after establishing the importance of barriers to entry, Greenwald and Kahn argue that there are really only three sustainable competitive advantages; 1. Supply. A company has this edge when it controls an important resource: A company may have a proprietary technology that is protected by a patent. 2. Demand. A company can control a market because customers are loyal to it, either out of habit - to a brand name, for example - or because the cost of switching to a different product is too high.

3. Economies of scale. If your operating costs remain fixed while output increases, you can gain a significant edge because you can offer your product at lower cost without sacrificing profit margins.

Having a superior competitive advantage of handsome retained earnings, a fine business selling in the market place for less than intrinsic value, should repurchase its shares at this lower market price. We can simply imagine the huge "Wall of China," and visualize it as a big barrier to entry. Such a barrier would be very expensive to reproduce. And, according to Professor Greenwald, the value of a strong brand barrier is equal to its "difficult for competitor to match" reproduction costs.[81] Using our experience and imagination to visualize competitive battles and historical campaigns can help us spot competitive strengths and weaknesses. We can also learn to recognize the opportunities and threats faced by winning and losing businesses.

Let's pause and see why it is wise to avoid the tough ones.[82]

In a difficult business, no sooner is one problem solved than another surfaces - never is there just one cockroach in the kitchen. Second, any initial advantage you secure will be quickly eroded by the low return that the business earns.

If you are right about a business whose value is largely dependent on a single key factor that is both easy to understand and enduring, the payoff is the same as if you had correctly analyzed an investment alternative characterized by constantly shifting and complex variables.

Charlie and I think we understand the company's economics and therefore believe we can make a reasonably intelligent guess about its future. However, we have no ability to forecast the economics of the investment banking business (in which we had a position through our 1987 purchase of Salomon convertible preferred), the airline industry, or the paper industry. This does not mean that we predict a negative future for these industries: we're agnostics, not atheists.

Warren Buffett

Excerpt: From the 1996 Letter, Buffett wrote about the Three Major Competitive Advantages of the Reinsurance Unit.[83]

In the super-cat business, we have three major competitive advantages. First, the parties buying reinsurance from us know that we both can and will pay under the most adverse of circumstances. Were a truly cataclysmic disaster to occur, it is not impossible that a financial panic would quickly follow. If that happened, there could well be respected reinsurers that would have difficulty paying at just the moment that their clients faced extraordinary needs. Indeed, one reason we never "lay off" part of

the risks we insure is that we have reservations about our ability to collect from others when disaster strikes. When it's Berkshire promising, insureds know with certainty that they can collect promptly.

Our second advantage - somewhat related - is subtle but important. After a mega-catastrophe, insurers might well find it difficult to obtain reinsurance even though their need for coverage would then be particularly great. At such a time, Berkshire would without question have very substantial capacity available - but it will naturally be our long-standing clients that have first call on it. That business reality has made major insurers and reinsurers throughout the world realize the desirability of doing business with us. Indeed, we are currently getting sizable "standby" fees from reinsurers that are simply nailing down their ability to get coverage from us should the market tighten.

Our final competitive advantage is that we can provide dollar coverages of a size neither matched nor approached elsewhere in the industry. Insurers looking for huge covers know that a single call to Berkshire will produce a firm and immediate offering.

QUOTE & CASE EXAMPLE FROM THE 2007 ANNUAL REPORT:[84]

Long-term competitive advantage in a stable industry is what we seek in a business. If that comes with rapid organic growth, great. But even without organic growth, such a business is rewarding. We will simply take the lush earnings of the business and use them to buy similar businesses elsewhere. There's no rule that you have to invest money where you've earned it. Indeed, it's often a mistake to do so: Truly great businesses, earning huge returns on tangible assets, can't for any extended period reinvest a large portion of their earnings internally at high rates of return.

Let's look at the prototype of a dream business, our own See's Candy. The boxed-chocolates industry in which it operates is unexciting: Per-capita consumption in the U.S. is extremely low and doesn't grow. Many once-important brands have disappeared, and only three companies have earned more than token profits over the last forty years. Indeed, I believe that See's, though it obtains the bulk of its revenues from only a few states, accounts for nearly half of the entire industry's earnings.

At See's, annual sales were 16 million pounds of candy when Blue Chip Stamps purchased the company in 1972. (Charlie and I controlled Blue Chip at the time and later merged it into Berkshire.) Last year See's sold 31 million pounds, a growth rate of only 2% annually. Yet its durable competitive advantage, built by the See's family over a 50-year period, and strengthened subsequently by Chuck Huggins and Brad Kinstler, has produced extraordinary results for Berkshire.

We bought See's for $25 million when its sales were $30 million and pre-tax earnings were less than $5 million. The capital then required to conduct the business was $8 million. (Modest seasonal debt was also needed for a few months each year.) Consequently, the company was earning 60% pre-tax on invested capital. Two factors helped to minimize the funds required for operations. First, the product was sold for cash, and that eliminated accounts receivable. Second, the production and distribution cycle was short, which minimized inventories.

Last year See's sales were $383 million, and pre-tax profits were $82 million. The capital now required to run the business is $40 million. This means we have had to reinvest only $32 million since 1972 to handle the modest physical growth – and somewhat immodest financial growth – of the business. In the meantime pre-tax earnings have totaled $1.35 billion. All of that, except for the $32 million, has been sent to Berkshire (or, in the early years, to Blue Chip). After paying corporate taxes on the profits, we have used the rest to buy other attractive businesses. Just as Adam and Eve kick-started an activity that led to six billion humans, See's has given birth to multiple new streams of cash for us. (The biblical command to "be fruitful and multiply" is one we take seriously at Berkshire.)

There aren't many See's in Corporate America. Typically, companies that increase their earnings from $5 million to $82 million require, say, $400 million or so of capital investment to finance their growth. That's because growing businesses have both working capital needs that increase in proportion to sales growth and significant requirements for fixed asset investments.

A company that needs large increases in capital to engender its growth may well prove to be a satisfactory investment. There is, to follow through on our example, nothing shabby about earning $82 million pre-tax on $400 million of net tangible assets. But that equation for the owner is vastly different from the See's situation. It's far better to have an ever-increasing stream of earnings with virtually no major capital requirements. Ask Microsoft or Google.

CHAPTER THREE OF FIVE:
ABLE AND TRUSTWORTHY MANAGERS

Filter Number Three:

Does the Business have Able and Trustworthy Managers?[85]

Since a business is made up of human beings, the human capital invested in these organizations is important for its success. As investors, we should look for able and trustworthy and effective leadership within these companies. We depend on a group of thoughtful managers who are able to consider their situations and make wise decisions.

You may wonder how to recognize an Able and Trustworthy Manager. It will not always be easy, but here are a few helpful clues. Able and Trustworthy Managers will build intrinsic value and competitive advantage. Able but greedy managers will steal from you. As a shareholder, and part owner of a business, do you want a manager taking more money from you than what was agreed upon in his or her contract? The non-expensing of stock options was just that. Expensing and forming a simple and clear reward plan based on individual performance is clearly more just.

Do you want a quick preliminary checklist for evaluating management? We can use this 4-step S.O.A.P. process that is taught to medical doctors; (Subjective, Objective, Assessment, Plan). And, we can use it as a screening tool for determining which teams to watch.

Subjective (feelings)	Do we like his/her leadership and communication style? She or he makes us feel good about their prospects. He or she warns us about their competitive challenges ahead. KLM; Kings, Likables, & Morons. Discard the bad ones quickly.
Objective (facts)	5-year R.O.E. is rising or falling? Free Cash Flow to the Firm is rising or falling? Actions to maintain or improve profit margins? Run your 4-Filters Formula Checklist.
Assessment (impression)	Is there enough here to watch this business; or mark it "Too Tough." Munger said that if it is "too tough" or "too complex," then it goes in the wastebasket.
Plan	1.Discard or Study (monitor) 2.Buy or Sell

Such an approach will make use of your feelings and facts. Next, imagine this scenario. Someday, able but greedy investing managers may try to steal from you, the Berkshire Hathaway Shareholder. The BRK.A "market price" may be sitting calm in the market waters at say "$500,000" for a couple of years. Some enterprising and able corporate raider team, backed by sovereign funds and big complex junk bonds, may arrive at our Berkshire Hathaway castle looking for booty. They will tell a good tale. We are here to break up the kingdom and "unlock value." That will be the telltale sign. What they will really mean is this: "We are here to break up the company into pieces, drive up the market price of each piece and make a bundle of loot for ourselves." Such pirates spread the cancer of fear into good businesses. Are they here to build intrinsic value or drive up market value? Our own managers will need to be able, trustworthy, owner-oriented, forward thinking, and strong of character.

One easy way to spot suboptimal or "bad" managers is to calculate what percentage of the operating profits they are being paid in total compensation. In the training of Family Physicians, they teach young doctors to have a "High Index of Suspicion" in formulating a differential diagnosis. As a shareholder, trust-but-verify that your managers are building "intrinsic value per share."[86] The market price will eventually follow. For, as a shareholder, and part owner of a fine business, do you want a manager taking more money from your pocket and putting it into his or her pocket? We want to be associated with builders of "intrinsic value" rather than takers of "market value." In evaluating business acquisition candidates, Warren Buffett and Charlie Munger want their businesses run by managers they like, admire, and trust.[87] Here are eleven factors from Phil Fisher to look for.

Eleven Management Related Factors edited from Phillip Fisher's 15 Questions Checklist:

2. Does the management have a determination to continue to develop products or processes that will further increase total sales potentials when the growth potentials of currently attractive product lines have largely been exploited?

3. How effective are the company's research and development efforts in relation to its size?

4. Does the company have an above-average sales organization?

6. What is the company doing to maintain or improve profit margins?

7. Does the company have outstanding labor and personnel relations?

8. Does the company have outstanding executive relations?

9.Does the company have depth to its management?

10.How good are the company's cost analysis and accounting controls?

12.Does the company have a short-range or long-range outlook in regard to profits?

14.Does the management talk freely to investors about its affairs when things are going well but "clam up" when troubles and disappointments occur?

15.Does the company have a management of unquestionable integrity?

Look for managers who have Integrity, Intelligence, Energy, and Enthusiasm. For more detailed examples, I refer you to Robert P. Miles book: The Warren Buffett CEO." Bob Miles discusses many of the business managers at Berkshire Hathaway in greater detail.[88] These managers must have the ability to allocate capital efficiently within their own businesses. In 1988, Buffett called seven business operations the "Sainted Seven": Buffalo News, Fechheimer, Kirby, Nebraska Furniture Mart, Scott Fetzer Manufacturing Group, See's, and World Book. "With no benefit from financial leverage, this group earned about 67% on average equity capital."[89] Warren Buffett described Berkshire Hathaway managers this way: "At Berkshire, our managers will continue to earn extraordinary returns from what appear to be ordinary businesses. These managers look for ways to deploy their earnings advantageously in their businesses. What's left, they will send to Charlie and me. We then try to use the funds in ways that build per-share intrinsic value." [90] From the 1995 Letter, notice this excerpt and restatement of goals: "Charlie Munger, Berkshire's Vice Chairman and my partner, and I want to build a collection of companies - both wholly- and partly-owned - that have excellent economic characteristics and that are run by outstanding managers."[91]

Warren Buffett, like Philip Fisher and others, believes that the ability of management can dramatically affect the equity "coupons."[92] He wrote that "the quality of management affects the bond coupon only when management is inept or dishonest that payment of interest is suspended." When buying businesses or common stocks, Buffett and Munger look for first-class businesses accompanied by first-class managements. These managers must also have the added ability to estimate loss costs. With businesses in property, casualty, and reinsurance, the problems of estimating potential loss is expanded. Wrote Buffett, "We achieved our gains through the efforts of a superb corps of operating managers who get extraordinary results from some ordinary-appearing businesses. Casey Stengel described managing a baseball team as "getting paid for home runs other fellows hit." The businesses in which we have partial interests are equally important to Berkshire's success."[93]

This 2000 letter excerpt is about their respect for the previous owners' prevailing operational style. "We find it meaningful when an owner cares about whom he sells to. We like to do business with someone who loves his business, not just the money that a sale will bring him (though we certainly understand why he likes that as well). When this emotional attachment exists, it signals that important qualities will likely be found within the business: honest accounting, pride of product, respect for customers, and a loyal group of associates having a strong sense of direction. The reverse is apt to be true, also. When an owner auctions off his business, exhibiting a total lack of interest in what follows, you will frequently find that it has been dressed up for sale, particularly when the seller is a "financial owner." And if owners behave with little regard for their business and its people, their conduct will often contaminate attitudes and practices throughout the company. When a business masterpiece has been created by a lifetime or several lifetimes of unstinting care and exceptional talent, it should be important to the owner what corporation is entrusted to carry on its history. Charlie and I believe Berkshire provides an almost unique home. We take our obligations to the people who created a business very seriously, and Berkshire's ownership structure ensures that we can fulfill our promises. When we (told) John Justin that his business will remain headquartered in Fort Worth, or assure the Bridge family that its operation will not be merged with another jeweler, these sellers can take those promises to the bank."[94]

Ben Graham also considered management. In his book "Security Analysis," Ben Graham admitted that it might be difficult to select unusually capable management. Since objective tests for management ability are rare, an investor often has to rely upon the reputation of a company's management. Graham was also aware of the psychological pressures facing managers. He made this comment about the temptation facing honest management: "While it should be emphasized that the overwhelming majority of managements are honest, it must be emphasized also that loose or "purposive" accounting is a highly contagious disease... Manipulation of the reported earnings by the management even for the desirable purpose of maintaining them on an even keel is objectionable none the less because it may too readily lead to manipulation for more sinister reasons."

The beauty of Munger's and Buffett's approach, of associating with "Able and Trustworthy Managers", is simplicity. Buffett and Munger do not have to coach great players at the peak of their games. And, since many of these businesses already have a winning strategy, there is no need to develop new strategies. However, these managers can turn to Buffett and Munger to redeploy earnings for higher returns. Warren Buffett wrote: "Low returns on corporate equity would suggest a very high dividend payout so that owners could direct capital toward more attractive areas."[95]

In summary, Able and Trustworthy Managers will build intrinsic value, but "able greedy managers" will steal from you. As you continue to build your own latticework of mental models and your own circle of competence, use Phil Fisher's filters when thinking about these examples and your own set of experiences. Integrate your own ideas in an organized and prioritized way. Now that we know filter number three is vital for business success, you and I can better learn to use both feelings and facts in sizing up managers.

Warren Buffett talking about Mrs. Rose Blumkin:[96]

She met every obstacle you would expect (and a few you wouldn't) when a business endowed with only $500 and no locational or product advantage goes up against rich, long-entrenched competition. At one early point, when her tiny resources ran out, "Mrs. B" coped in a way not taught at business schools: she simply sold the furniture and appliances from her home in order to pay creditors precisely as promised.

One question I always ask myself in appraising a business is how I would like, assuming I had ample capital and skilled personnel, to compete with it. I'd rather wrestle grizzlies than compete with Mrs. B and her progeny. They buy brilliantly, they operate at expense ratios competitors don't even dream about, and they then pass on to their customers much of the savings.

On the topic of Candor, in 1996, Warren Buffett…

"We will be candid in our reporting to you, emphasizing the pluses and minuses important in appraising business value. Our guideline is to tell you the business facts that we would want to know if our positions were reversed. We owe you no less. Moreover, as a company with a major communications business, it would be inexcusable for us to apply lesser standards of accuracy, balance and incisiveness when reporting on ourselves than we would expect our news people to apply when reporting on others. We also believe candor benefits us as managers: the CEO who misleads others in public may eventually mislead himself in private."[97]

What I Learned Before I Sold to Warren Buffett: An Entrepreneur's Guide to Developing a Highly Successful Company. Barnett C. Helzberg, Jr [98]

When he bought us, Buffett's empire of 22,000 associates was overseen by only 11 people at his Omaha head-quarters. No micromanagement there. And talk about trust. Explaining how he makes this hands-off approach work, Buffett said that it was "because the managers operate with total autonomy and they do such a terrific job we really don't need anyone to supervise them. Managers run their own shows. They don't have to report to central management," he said. "When we get somebody who is a .400 hitter we don't start telling them how to swing."

Concentrating on winners will help maximize your profits and make your life a whole lot more fun. What greater excitement than riding those winners to the finish line and getting that garland of roses? It sure beats moving poor performers up to mediocre.

Focus is your lever to success. As the leader you need to be sure you and your team are doing the right things, and as managers they need to be doing things right. Doing the right things is the leadership component—that is clearly up to you. The doing things right component is the province of the managers to whom you have delegated the responsibility. Anything that decreases focus on these right things inhibits progress. Investing unlimited effort in failing projects does not create success.

Do not underestimate the incredible amount of mental discipline it takes to focus yourself and your teammates. Wonderful alternatives and seductive opportunities abound and temptations to go in multiple directions are unlimited. Of course, consistently working on the basics can get boring, especially when things are going well. Why not open a print shop or sign shop, do your own payroll, or engage in a myriad of services to save money? **Such temptations take you away from the constant improvement needed in your core business to be the best in your industry.**

Commit yourself to be the best, define what that means, and focus on the head of that pin like no one in your industry. Have a clear simple objective, let your team develop the road-map, and go for it!

Example from the 1987 Letter of the "Able and Trustworthy," Harry Bottle.

Buffett wrote: "Some of these former partners will remember that in 1962 I encountered severe managerial problems at Dempster Mill Manufacturing

Co., a pump and farm implement manufacturing company that BPL controlled.

At that time, like now, I went to Charlie with problems that were too tough for me to solve. Charlie suggested the solution might lie in a California friend of his, Harry Bottle, whose special knack was never forgetting the fundamental. I met Harry in Los Angeles on April 17, 1962, and on April 23 he was in Beatrice, Nebraska, running Dempster. Our problems disappeared almost immediately. In my 1962 annual letter to partners, I named Harry "Man of the Year."

Fade to 24 years later: The scene is K & W Products, a small Berkshire subsidiary that produces automotive compounds. For years K & W did well, but in 1985-86 it stumbled badly, as it pursued the unattainable to the neglect of the achievable.

Charlie, who oversees K & W, knew there was no need to consult me. Instead, he called Harry, now 68 years old, made him CEO, and sat back to await the inevitable. He didn't wait long. In 1987 K & W's profits set a record, up more than 300% from 1986. And, as profits went up, capital employed went down: K & W's investment in accounts receivable and inventories has decreased 20%. If we run into another managerial problem ten or twenty years down the road, you know whose phone will ring."

(Harry Bottle is mentioned in both the 1987 and 1989 letters.)

CHAPTER FOUR OF FIVE:
BARGAIN PRICE IS A MARGIN OF SAFETY

Filter Number Four:

Is the Business available at a Bargain Price?

"Margin of Safety" has been called the three most important words in investing by Benjamin Graham and Warren Buffett.[99] This is the final and pivotal filter of the Four Filters Formula. Here we estimate or calculate an estimated intrinsic value for the stock or for the whole company as a business. Once we know the estimated intrinsic value, we can compare that figure with the market price and see if we are getting a bargain. If we are getting a bargain, this bargain is our Margin of Safety.

Think about the Great Depression and the bursting of technology and housing bubbles, and you get the idea. We need a method of insuring safety. Like we warn our children: "Safety First. Safety First." Purchasing something at a bargain price gives us a "margin of safety." It opens up the opportunity of using our remaining funds to purchase something else. It helps to protect us from market fluctuations and foolish losses. Warren Buffett and

Charlie Munger believe this margin-of-safety principle, strongly emphasized by Ben Graham, is the cornerstone of investment success.[100]

After judging quality, how do we decide what price is a bargain? Warren Buffett says that most analysts feel they must choose between two approaches: value and growth.[101] In Buffett and Munger's opinion, growth is a component in the calculation of value. Buffett said, ".. as one variable used in the calculation of value, growth's importance can range from negligible to enormous. And, growth can be both negative as well as positive."

You may wonder who came up with a formal way to calculate and reasonably estimate value. In 1938, John Burr Williams described the equation for value in his book, "The Theory of Investment Value."[102] Buffett summarized this as: "The value of any stock, bond, or business today is determined by the cash inflows and outflows - discounted at an appropriate interest rate - that can be expected to occur during the remaining life of the asset." Why discounted back to the present? Discount it back to the present because, over time, inflation tends to decrease the dollar's purchasing power. Later in this chapter, I demonstrate an "intrinsic value" estimation for you.

In that section of his Chairman's Letter on "price attractiveness," Warren Buffett wrote "the (valuation) formula is the same for stocks as it is for bonds. Even so, there is an important, and difficult to deal with, difference between the two. A bond has a coupon and maturity date that define future cash flows; but, in the case of equities, the investment analyst must himself estimate the future "coupons."[103] At the moment of purchase, will the market present you with value at a bargain price? The big idea here is to look at a reasonable intrinsic value first. Think about the intrinsic value. Next, think about the price you are willing to pay to obtain that much value. In valuing a business as a whole, the main issue should not be about P/E (price to earnings) or P/B (price to book) or the Dividend Yield component. The main issue in business valuation is about finding and estimating the P/V (price to value ratio). This relative relationship of the intrinsic value of the business to the value obtained upon purchase is important. In fact, Warren Buffett said that a high ratio of price to book value, a high price-earnings ratio, and a low dividend yield; are in no way inconsistent with a value purchase.[104]

Then, looking forward in time, estimating the value of future coupons of a business can deceptively pull us off the reality track. My job here is to help steer us on the better path to an intrinsic value estimation. And, my rediscovery of the Buffett and Munger invention (The Four Filters) can help us do this nicely.

Recall that Warren Buffett warns us that we can easily go wrong in estimating future "coupons." At Berkshire Hathaway, Mr. Buffett attempts to deal with this estimation problem in two ways. Here, I take the liberty of breaking up his quote into two distinct sections so that you can better visualize the qualitative and quantitative components of the Four Filters as a formula.[105]

"First, we try to stick to businesses we believe we understand.
That means they must be relatively simple and stable in
character. If a business is complex or subject to constant change,
we're not smart enough to predict future cash flows. Incidentally,
that shortcoming doesn't bother us. What counts for most people
in investing is not how much they know, but rather how
realistically they define what they don't know. An investor needs
to do very few things right as long as he or she avoids big

mistakes."

Using the Four Filters as a "Time Travel" instrument, imagine what has worked in the past and imagine what principles can work in the future. You will see that the quote above can be reinterpreted to encompass the qualitative filters of: 1.Understanding, 2.Sustainable Competitive Advantage, 3.Able & Trustworthy Managers. Filters 1 to 3 set up a more stable qualitative candidate or prospect for doing a "discounted free cash flow" quantitative intrinsic value estimation. This is the beauty of the Four Filters innovation. It is an effective algorithm that combines qualitative and quantitative factors. See that the quote below refers to the fourth and final filter: 4. Margin of Safety given by a Bargain Price.

"Second, and equally important, we insist on a margin of safety in our purchase price. If we calculate the value of a common stock to be only slightly higher than its price, we're not interested in buying. We believe this margin-of-safety principle, so strongly emphasized by Ben Graham, to be the cornerstone of investment success."

Now, if the investment prospect has passed the "Four Filter" test of Understanding, Sustainable Competitive Advantage, and Able Trustworthy Managers, let's estimate a quantitative intrinsic value. That way we can estimate how much of a bargain we might be getting. Interestingly, Charlie Munger once stated: "Warren often talks about these discounted cash flows, but I've never seen him do one." Warren Buffett responded: "Its sort of automatic... It ought to just kind of scream at you that you've got this huge margin of safety."[106] Buffett went on to state: "We define intrinsic value as the discounted value of the cash that can be taken out of a business during its remaining life. Anyone calculating intrinsic value necessarily comes up with a highly subjective figure. This figure will change both as estimates of future cash flows are revised and as interest rates move. Despite its fuzziness, however, intrinsic value is all-important and is the only logical way to evaluate the relative attractiveness of investments and businesses."

In estimating "Intrinsic Value," I like the logical stepwise approach of Professor Bruce C.N. Greenwald of Columbia University. In his book, *Value Investing. From Graham to*

Buffett and Beyond," he and Judd Kahn have a rational approach to valuation.[107] They take us sequentially from valuing real physical assets first, then to valuing basic earning power second. Third, they calculate (estimate) the value of growth. They teach a company-centric three stage valuation method. It is based on a grasp of the economic situation in which the business finds itself. It puts more emphasis on information about the firm that is solid and certain. This approach forces the student to think more rationally. This three stage method is based on three elements: the value of the assets, earnings power value, and the value of growth.

1. Value of the Assets: First, start with the balance sheet, which tells us what the business is worth. Remember that many of the stated valuations owe more to accounting conventions than to what the assets could actually fetch in the real-life transactions. So, make the adjustments needed to align the official numbers to real-world values. Working from the top of the balance sheet to the bottom, progress from valuation questions that are easy like cash, to those that are difficult, such as goodwill or physical plant. Replace book numbers with more realistic alternatives such as liquidation cost or replacement cost.

2. Earnings Power Value: The earnings power value (EPV) of a firm assumes zero growth. EPV is computed using the following formula. EPV = AE/R where AE = adjusted earnings and R = required return or cost of capital. Note four adjustments we make to earnings:

a. Eliminate nonrecurring items.
b. Align depreciation expense with what the company really has to spend to maintain the physical assets.
c. Account for the fact that the earnings estimate may reflect a time in the business cycle at an unsustainably high or low point. So, increase or decrease the reported figure and get a more representative picture of the company's normal level of performance.
d. Allow for the value of a "franchise," if any.

We expect EPV to confirm and be equal to the asset-based valuation. If EPV is less, it means management needs to do more to generate profit. If EPV exceeds asset value, determine whether the difference is supported by a special "franchise" that will prevent competitors from chipping away until the company's EPV is equal to asset value.

3. Estimated Value of Growth: Greenwald and Kahn isolate the "Growth" estimation for two reasons. First, growth involves assumptions less reliable. Second, the only kind of growth worth incorporating into stock valuation is growth where the increase in earnings exceeds the additional capital necessary to support the new business. If we get this far, evaluate the business's competitive franchise and build in a margin of safety to accommodate uncertainties in this area. The margin of future uncertainty is based on the extent to which the present value of projected cash flows exceeds the EPV. Remember that Earnings Power Value, EPV, assumes zero or no growth. At this point, we may add variables incorporating expected growth estimations to the EPV computation.

Let's take a look at a simple and recent "valuation of assets" example. I think this example will also give us an idea of what a hypothetical competitor would need to do. Recently, The Pritzker family decided to gradually sell or reorganize some of its holdings including the Marmon Group of Companies.[108] Marmon is a company operating 125 businesses in nine industrial sectors. Its largest operation is Union Tank Car, which together with a Canadian counterpart owns 94,000 rail cars that are leased to various shippers. The original cost of this fleet is $5.1 billion. In addition, Marmon has $7 billion in annual sales and about 20,000 employees. Berkshire Hathaway will soon purchase 60% of Marmon and will acquire virtually all of the balance within six years. Berkshire's initial outlay will be $4.5 billion, and the price of the remaining purchase will be based on a formula tied to earnings.

For fun, imagine being a competitor, and lets do a fair "replacement cost" estimate just on the 94,000 railcars alone. By doing this we get a sense as to whether Berkshire Hathaway is getting a bargain. Multiply 94,000 rail cars times what? Made out of steel, the boxcar cost about $45,000 a copy in 1980. Research revealed that $90,000 would be a fair price to pay for a mid-age mid-use rail car which can be depreciated over about 40-50 years. So, 94,000 x $90,000 = $8.46 Billion just in railcars alone. Furthermore, consider that the Marmon Group is composed of 125 different companies. And, I may be understating the replacement cost of a mid-age, mid-use rail car.

So, sensible bargain purchases need not involve complex math. Members of the Pritzker family would be wise to turn around and buy some undervalued Berkshire Hathaway stock.

Case Example: Intrinsic Value Estimation of Kraft (KFT)

Why did Berkshire Hathaway buy stock in Kraft? Let's examine the possible reasons together. What did they understand about this company? Brands? Costs Controls? Expanding Markets? Share Buybacks? Chairman Irene Rosenfeld?

Berkshire Hathaway, recently bought more than 132 million shares of food company Kraft, according to a document filed with the Securities and Exchange Commission. Kraft Foods Inc. (KFT), through its subsidiaries, is engaged in the manufacture and sale of packaged foods and beverages in the United States, Canada, Europe, Latin America, Asia Pacific, the Middle East and Africa. Kraft manufactures and markets packaged food products, consisting principally of beverages, cheese, snacks, convenient meals and various packaged grocery products. The Company operates in two segments: Kraft North America Commercial and Kraft International Commercial. It has operations in 72 countries and sells its products in more than 155 countries.

Kraft Foods Inc. began in 1903 as a cheese manufacturer. The company is now the largest North America-based food and

beverage company and the second largest in the world after Nestlé SA. From 1988 to March of 2007, tobacco giant Phillip Morris Company, now Altria Group (MO), owned and grew Kraft Foods, merging the food company with Nabisco and General Foods. In 1985, Berkshire Hathaway benefitted from owning shares in General Foods. Altria Group (MO) took Kraft public in 2001, maintaining an 88.1% stake in the stock until the completion of the spin off in 2007.

First, understand that **Kraft has nine brands with revenues exceeding $1 billion**: Kraft cheeses, dinners and dressings; Oscar Mayer meats; Philadelphia cream cheese; Maxwell House coffee; Nabisco cookies and crackers and its Oreo brand; Jacobs coffees, Milka chocolates and LU biscuits. Kraft has more than 50 additional brands with revenues of at least $100 million. Respected brands can translate into some measure of pricing power.

Kraft Foods, KFT has a (5-year annual average) net income growth rate of negative 4.71 . The company is looking forward to a 7-9% forward growth rate. What competitive advantages does it have? Brands, Technology, Cost of Production, Distribution Network? Kraft sells its products in more than 155 countries. Are possible advantages sustainable? Kraft is a major purchaser of milk, cheese, plastic, nuts, green coffee beans, cocoa, corn products, wheat, pork, poultry, beef, vegetable oil, sugar, other sweeteners and numerous other commodities. If Kraft is unable to increase its prices to offset increased cost of commodities, Kraft Foods can also experience lower profitability.

It's market price is 29.31 at the time of this writing. The estimated Intrinsic Value, using an assumed 7% forward growth rate, is 43.39 per share from the discounted cash flow process used at ValuePro.net, and this may or may not indicate a bargain of 14 dollars. If the 7% growth assumptions used in estimating the Intrinsic Value are accurate and sustainable, this may or may not indicate a price-to-value ratio of .67 , and a possible "margin of safety" of 33 percent in a good business with good brands selling at a fair price. Notice that the $43 estimate is close to the $44 intrinsic value estimate based on cash flows that we will perform together at the end of this section.

Is it a possible Value Trap? While this is always one possibility when buying an assumed bargain, I think this is more likely to be a safe play because Kraft appears to pass the first three filters of understanding, enduring competitive advantages, and able trustworthy managers. While Kraft's current price/earnings ratio = 18.2, remember that we are more concerned with a price/intrinsic value ratio. Kraft's current return on capital is a sluggish 5.41.

Using a debt to equity ratio of .77, Kraft Foods shows a current return on equity = 9.32 Some industries have higher ROE because they require no assets, such as consulting firms. Other industries require large infrastructure builds before they generate a penny of profit. Generally, capital-intensive businesses have higher barriers to entry, which limit competition. Also, high-ROE firms with small asset bases tend to have lower barriers to entry. Thus, such firms face more business risk because competitors can replicate their success without having to obtain much outside funding.

Note my automatic warning, (above 0.5), on this current debt to equity level of .77 . KFT pays an annual dividend of $1.08 per share. DY (Dividend Yield): DY reflects dividend per share as a percent of Price. Kraft has a Dividend Yield of 3.6%.

From 2007 excerpts, the company expects that revenue will grow 3% to 4% on an organic basis in 2008 and that "we'll hit our stride" by 2009, said Chief Executive Irene Rosenfeld in a written release. "We'll fully realize the financial benefits of our investments and deliver our long-term targets of at least 4% organic net revenue growth and 7% to 9% EPS growth." In addition to "rewiring" the company, Rosenfeld said Kraft intends to "reframe" its product categories to make them more relevant to consumers, to better exploit its sales abilities and to drive down costs.

One key is to expand the focus in larger, faster-growing categories. As an example, Rosenfeld cited moving away from dying sectors like processed cheese slices and into sandwich, snacking and high-end cheeses. Also important is grabbing market share away from restaurants, she said, vowing that Kraft will strive to provide "restaurant-quality food at home in the office or anywhere ... at a fraction of the cost." Frozen pizza's a case in point.

With brands like Jacks' and Tombstone, Kraft has long been a major player in the $4 billion category. Then, about 10 years ago it went after the $11 billion chain business with higher-end offerings like DiGiorno. And now, Rosenfeld said, "we are setting our sights on the $20 billion local pizzeria" category.

Does Kraft Foods make for an intelligent investment or speculation today? Time is said to be the friend of the wonderful business and the enemy of the mediocre one. Before making an investment decision, use the four filters. Seek an understanding about the company, its products, and its sustainable competitive advantages over competitors. Next, look for able and trustworthy managers who are focused more on value than just growth. Finally ask: Is there a bargain relative to its intrinsic value per share today? I use it as a case example here to illustrate one way of calculating and estimating an intrinsic value based on free cash flows.

You may wonder how to do an intrinsic value estimation on your own. Here I present an estimation example that is based just on Kraft's projected free cash flows. However, keep in mind that valuation is a holistic process that should also consider the value of competitive advantages and the first three filters. Before proceeding, recall the three steps presented in the value investing course at Columbia University.

1. Net Asset Value (Business Reproduction Costs)

Subtract liabilities from assets to get net asset value. Using this valuation method, the intrinsic value of the company is its net asset value. Benjamin Graham only considered current assets (cash, accounts receivable, inventory, etc.)   In contrast, contemporary value investors may include plant, property, equipment and sometimes the intangibles. In this example. I substitute the book value per share for Kraft of $17.80

2. Earnings Power Value (Cash Flow Value Without Growth)
The basic formula for earnings power value is given as follows. Earnings Power Value = (Adjusted Earnings)(1/Cost of Capital). Before calculating earnings power value, we need to know two terms: adjusted earnings and cost of capital. Adjusted earnings are a company's normalized earnings, i.e., earnings stripped of one-time charges, depreciation, and/or unstainable peak or trough earnings figures. A riskier asset will require a higher interest rate. The Cost of Capital is also called the "discount rate."
Net Income $2,590/.06 = 43,166.67
$43,166.67 / 1,522 = $28.36

Definition: Estimated Franchise Value = (EPV – Net Asset Value)
Estimated Franchise Value = ($28.36 - 17.80) = $10.56

3. Growth Component

The growth value of a company is very difficult to nail down with precision. So, this uncertainty makes "growth value" the least reliable indicator of a company's intrinsic value. V of growth = Dividends / (R – G). The Value of growth is equal to the dividend cash flows discounted back to the present.

In the case of Kraft, growth may come from developing markets around the world. Let's take a look at the "Valuation of the Growth Component" using the discounting of 10 year Free Cash Flows. Free cash flow, (FCF), is more difficult to manipulate than net income because it is the amount of cash remaining after accounting for current expenses.

(FCF = Net Income + Depreciation/Amortization - Changes In Working Capital - Capital Expenditure) or, summarized as (FCFF = NOP – Taxes – Net Investment – Net Change in Working Capital).

Keep in mind that the stage one evaluation, in the Value Investing book of Greenwald and Kahn, is focused on Kraft's assets. Next, their stage two valuation is focused on Kraft's EPV, or Earnings Power Value, without any assumptions of growth.

Stage Three is an estimation of the growth component using free cash flows. In order to arrive at a reasonable figure, we assume here that management's expectation of 7% to 9% EPS growth is reasonable and achievable. Using a starting Free Cash Flow of $3,571.00 in 2007, and growing at 7% and 8% for the designated years 1-4 and 5-7 as shown in the table below, each cash flow amount grows at either the 7% o 8% assumed growth rate. We use a 10 year span to arrive at an estimated intrinsic value per share, after we have discounted each of these flows using the 6% discount rate.

Our estimation assumes that the number of shares outstanding will stay constant. If Kraft were to buy back shares in the future, without incurring additional debt, this would have a positive effect upon the value of each share. Next, notice in the table below that these future cash flows are discounted back individually to present values using a 6% cost of capital assumption. This results in an estimated intrinsic value of $26.59 based on the free cash growth component. When added to the present book value per share of $17.80 the combined intrinsic value per share is an estimated $44.39 using these assumptions.

Year	FCF	PV of FCF	PV COH		
Start	$ 3,571.00	$ 3,571.00	239.00	Starting Cash On Hand	$ 239.00
1	3,820.97	3,604.69	225.47	Starting FCF	$ 3,571.00
2	4,088.44	3,638.70	212.71	Next Year Growth	7%
3	4,374.63	3,673.02	200.67	Year 2 - 4	7%
4	4,680.85	3,707.67	189.31	Year 5 - 7	8%
5	5,055.32	3,777.63	178.59	Year 8 - 10	7%
6	5,459.75	3,848.91	168.49	Discount Rate	6%
7	5,896.53	3,921.53	158.95	Shares Outstanding in Year 1	1,522.0
8	6,309.28	3,958.52	149.95	Shares Outstaning Compound Rate (Optional)	0%
9	6,750.93	3,995.87	141.46		
10	7,223.50	4,033.56	133.46	Year 10 PV Price	40,469.09
year 10 sale price	72,234.98	40,335.64		Year 10 Shares Outstanding	1522.0
year 10 cash on	239.00	133.46		Est. Intrinsic Value / Share based on proj.	$26.59

hand				Free Cash Flow	
year 10 sale price	72,473.98	40,469.09		Book Value / share	$17.80
					$44.39

Since the market price of Kraft is $29.31 at the time of this writing, and the intrinsic value estimate is around $40 per share, we are getting a nice bargain in a business with attractive brands. If the growth assumptions used in estimating the intrinsic value are accurate and sustainable, this may or may not indicate a price-to-value ratio of .73 , and a possible margin of safety of approximately 27 percent. I believe that this case section has given you some of the important reasons why Berkshire Hathaway invested in Kraft.

In terms of Opportunity Cost, is Kraft the best place to invest our money today? I do not know enough about Kraft, but I am open to talking and discussing KFT further. The answer to this capital allocation question is a personal one. It should be based upon our circle of competence. After we have analyzed several businesses using the Four Filters process, we can make this allocation decision more easily. We will have more subjective and objective information in our mental models that will help us make an informed decision. Then, based on both our feelings and our facts, we decide which choices will make for better returns on our investments. The Four Filters are a set of tools that can help us make wiser investing decisions. In this chapter we have seen that we can use simple math to estimate an intrinsic value. Thanks to Benjamin Graham, knowing the estimated intrinsic value of a business helps us avoid situations that do not present a margin of safety.

CHAPTER FIVE OF FIVE: SUMMARY

As significant as the refinement of the microscope by Antonie van Leeuwenhoek.[109]

I believe that Warren Buffett and Charlie Munger invented an investing formula that is underappreciated by the business and academic communities. The Four Filters process is an effective intellectual achievement in both practical and Behavioral Finance. The Four Filters are an important set of steps used by the world's greatest investors. They function as an effective time-tested focusing formula for investing success. They serve as a very useful guide for assessing intrinsic value and sensible price.

Behavioral Finance[110] and Common Sense have shown us that we all have human tendencies to frame ideas that are affected by our emotions. Ideally, we would use the best of our emotional and intellectual energies in the right way. The Four Filters reduce the risk of investment failure by helping us steer a better path to a quality bargain.

Charlie Munger has spoken about the merits of having a "pilot's checklist."[111] This is something I did not appreciate until I studied the Four Filters. These days, Warren Buffett mentioned the Four Filters in the 2007 annual report this way: "Charlie and I look for companies that have a) a business we understand; b) favorable long-term economics; c) able and trustworthy management; and d) a sensible price tag."[112] These Four Filters can enhance the probability of our investment success. They will help you in your search for intrinsic value and sensible investment.

In the 1985 Chairman's letter to Shareholders, Warren Buffett wrote that his advantage was attitude. The 2007 annual letter shows Buffett in top form, buying quality bargains. He learned from Ben Graham that the key to successful investing was the purchase of shares in good businesses when market prices were at a large discount from underlying business values. Along the way, he and Charlie Munger got better at picking stocks and whole companies for investment. Their experience and an expanded knowledge base helped them look for understandable first-class businesses with enduring competitive advantages. Philip Fisher and others have influenced their views on evaluating first-class managements and evaluating a business's growth potential.[113]

Note however that growth is only one component in assessing value. Through the conscientious process of Elaboration and Elimination, the Four Filters illuminate the most important factors for business and investing success. The Four Filters highlight and reveal the good prospects and eliminate the bad prospects for investment. They encompass four clusters that are vitally important to investing success: 1. Products 2. Customers 3. Management 4. Margin of Safety. In each of these four clusters, we can imagine the influence of Ben Graham, Philip Fisher, Charles Munger, and John Burr Williams. Business students can also imagine the ideas of Porter and Greenwald in these filters. The development of this Four Filters Formula has probably been an evolutionary process. And, by 1977, the Four Filters were being used like a "checklist" by our pilots, Warren Buffett and Charlie Munger. You can read about many of these influences in Andy Kilpatrick's big comprehensive book, "Of Permanent Value: The Story of Warren Buffett."

If Buffett and Munger had focused solely on the fourth filter, "Margin of Safety" from bargain prices, they would have still done well. However, used as a sequential set of filters, the Four Filters Formula is remarkably effective in preventing loss. It is an elegant algorithm that combines the use of important qualitative and quantitative decision steps. Warren Buffett has also phrased the Four Filter check points in this way: "When buying companies or common stocks, we look for understandable first-class businesses, with enduring competitive advantages, accompanied by first-class managements, available at a bargain price."

From a historical point of view, the record at Berkshire Hathaway under Warren Buffett's tenure speaks for itself. Over the last 43 years, Berkshire Hathaway's book value has grown from $19 to $78,008, a rate of 21.1% compounded annually. Berkshire Hathaway's A share is selling at around $140,000 at the time of this writing (March, 2008). Its intrinsic value per share is much higher. And, it's future earning prospects look bright. Future investment managers will do well to practice owner-oriented business principles. I hope Future investment managers understand the effectiveness of this "Four Filter" formula. I practice the Four Filters process.

From a mathematical point of view, think of each stop along the Four Filters as a mutually exclusive and additive event. If a business passes a couple of filters, it is, by the process of elimination, farther to the right on a normal distribution curve. Of course, this filtering is from an "investment prospect" point of view. If this were a field of racing horses, movement along each step of the Four Filters path, the prospect enters a subset of "better than average" horse. Practicing these steps will make you a better investment thinker.

From a practical point of view, business is about taking good care of your customer and arriving at an agreeable trade. Finding the company that has enduring competitive advantage means that you are finding a business that has been tested by time and its customers. Products, Customers, Good Management, and Financial Safety given by a bargain purchase are always important. However, Charlie Munger has said that "people calculate too much and think too little."[114] Here, the filters guide our thinking on a sequential path to understanding. Working together, Buffett and Munger have produced a remarkable and effective Behavioral Finance formula. And, within that Fourth Filter, Bargain Price, we see Ben Graham's three most important words in investing, "Margin of Safety." So, investing safety is practically insured by purchasing at a bargain price.

Pricing Bubbles, Market excesses, and Government excesses will come and go. Warren Buffett wrote that a different set of major shocks is sure to occur in the future and that he will not try to predict these nor to profit from them. However, if he can identify businesses similar to those he has purchased in the past, external surprises will have little effect on long-term results. Buffett said: "We will stick with the approach that got us here and try not to relax our standards." In my own work, I will continue to use the Four Filters. In talking with students about focus, Warren Buffett often uses this baseball analogy using the story of Ted Williams and his book: "The Story of My Life." Buffett explained: "My argument is, to be a good hitter, you've got to get a good ball to hit. It's the first rule in the book. If I have to bite at stuff that is out of my happy zone, I'm not a .344 hitter. I might only be a .250 hitter." Charlie and I agree and (we) will try to wait for opportunities that are well within our own "happy zone.""

I have lost money foolishly and ignorantly, and did not like it. I have been an investing "innocent", and did not like that either. This stuff makes better sense. It helps us avoid the biggest investing risk: "The risk of losing money!" These four sequential steps to a better decision making process might have saved some recently collapsed Wall Street businesses.[115] The Four Filters process can help us impose a greater prudence upon our investment decision making. Writing about speculation, Ben Graham believed that the value of analysis diminishes as the element of chance increases. However, if we decrease the element of chance, imagine what this does for our predictive probabilities. We can continue to learn from the best. And, we can develop a better network of good information and scuttlebutt. By studying business situations more rationally, we can improve our decision making skills. Using the Four Filters, we can decrease the element of chance and increase our probability of focusing and finding a quality bargain.

As significant as the refinement of the microscope, I believe that Warren Buffett and Charlie Munger invented an investing formula that has worked effectively for over 31 years. They use ethics, time, training, psychology, and experiences to their advantage as well. I believe that the Four Filters Process incorporates their owner-oriented business principles into an easy to remember, "rational four steps guide." The Four Filters will help you get closer to your own "happy zone." Used carefully, it will help us avoid losing money. It has helped me greatly in my own investment decision thinking and my own investment decision making. Moreover, it can help us make better investing decisions. As Ben Graham said in the introduction of his book, *The Intelligent Investor*: "No statement is more true and better applicable to Wall Street than the famous warning of Santayana: "Those who do not remember the past are condemned to repeat it." I hope you have found value in my book. I welcome your feedback.

ADDITIONAL RESOURCES

Warren Buffett:

"An investor cannot obtain superior profits from stocks by simply committing to a specific investment category or style. He or she can earn them only by carefully evaluating facts and continuously exercising discipline."

Charlie Munger:

"They're radically different. Derivatives are full of clauses that say if one party's credit gets downgraded, then they have to put up collateral. It's like margin – you can go broke."[116]

"The way to win is to work, work, work, work and hope to have a few insights…. And you're probably not going to be smart enough to find thousands in a lifetime. And when you get a few, you really load up. It's just that simple."[117]

In 1996, Warren Buffett wrote this about investing in public companies. It is a twist on the Four Filter formula that sets the bar towards realism and conservativism:

"The art of investing in public companies successfully is little different from the art of successfully acquiring subsidiaries. In each case you simply want to acquire, at a sensible price, a business with excellent economics and able, honest management. Thereafter, you need only monitor whether these qualities are being preserved."[118]

LEARNING FROM EXPERIENCE:

"After many years of buying and supervising a great variety of businesses, Charlie and I have not learned how to solve difficult business problems. What we have learned is to avoid them. To the extent we have been successful, it is because we concentrated on identifying one-foot hurdles that we could step over rather than because we acquired any ability to clear seven-footers. The finding may seem unfair, but in both business and investments it is usually far more profitable to simply stick with the easy and obvious than it is to resolve the difficult. On occasion, tough problems must be tackled as was the case when we started our Sunday paper in Buffalo. In other instances, a great investment opportunity occurs when a marvelous business encounters a one-time huge, but solvable, problem as was the case many years back at both American Express and GEICO. Overall, however, we've done better by avoiding dragons than by slaying them."

On the issue of optimism and sensibility, why go conservatively?

People who have a rosy outlook are more likely than others to make prudent financial decisions, but those who are extreme optimists make riskier investments and save less money than others, a new study finds.[119] Manju Puri and David Robinson, professors of finance at Duke University in Durham, N.C., compared statistical and self-reported life expectancies to determine people's levels of optimism. Participants who expected to live an average of 20 years longer than is statistically likely were labeled "extreme optimists." In moderation, optimism can lead to sensible decision making, but extreme optimists "display financial habits and behavior that are generally not considered prudent," the authors write in the October issue of the Journal of Financial Economics.

This "Evolution of Value Investing" chart was modified from the original work of Lawrence Cunningham.[120]

http://deepwealth.blogspot.com/2006/02/traditions-in-value-investing.html

Investor		Key Points	
John Burr Williams	Discounted cash flow analysis	Focus on cash	The Theory of Investment Value
Ben Graham	Father of value of investing	Margin of safety; focus on balance sheet; 10-point checklist	The Intelligent Investor; Security Analysis; The Interpretation of Financial Statements
Phil Carret	12 Commandments of Investing":	Ignore mechanical formulas.	The Art of Speculation
Phil Fisher	Qualitative dimension, growth role	Scuttlebutt; focus on earnings; 15-point checklist	Common Stocks and Uncommon Profits
Howard Buffett	Morality and Human Nature	Greatest influence on Warren Buffett	
Charlie Munger	"The Wonderful Business" and the Latticework of "Mental Models"	**The Four Filters Invention**	Damn Right by Janet Lowe. Poor Charlie's Almanack by Peter Kaufman.
Warren Buffett	Circle of competence business analysis		The Owner's Manual and the Annual Letters to Shareholders
Bill Ruane	Trusted friend of Buffett.	Buffett recommended him to partners in 1969.	The Sequoia Fund
Lou Simpson	Buffett's first choice.	"independent thinker"	Record speaks for itself.
Ajit Jain	Reinsurance and Risk Wizard	"limiter of risk exposure"	Reinsurance Record speaks for itself.

1994 excerpt and another example of the Four Filters:

Warren Buffett: We believe that **our formula** - the purchase at sensible prices of businesses that have good underlying economics and are run by honest and able people - is certain to produce reasonable success. We expect, therefore, to keep on doing well.

A fat wallet, however, is the enemy of superior investment results...Though there are as many good businesses as ever, it is useless for us to make purchases that are inconsequential in relation to Berkshire's capital... Berkshire's investment universe has shrunk dramatically.

Most folks agree that the majority of Berkshire Hathaway businesses have important competitive advantages that will endure over time. For Warren Buffett and his shareholders, it is comforting to be in businesses where some mistakes can be made and yet satisfactory overall performance can be achieved.[121]..."We ordinarily make no attempt to buy equities for anticipated favorable stock price behavior in the short term. In fact, if their business experience continues to satisfy us, we welcome lower market prices of stocks we own as an opportunity to acquire even more of a good thing at a better price." Warren Buffett[122]

"I could give you other personal examples of "bargain-purchase" folly but I'm sure you get the picture: It's far better to buy a wonderful company at a fair price than a fair company at a wonderful price. Charlie understood this early; I was a slow learner. But now, when buying companies or common stocks, we look for first-class businesses accompanied by first-class managements." [123] Warren Buffett

Friend and Author of "Getting Started in Value Investing," Charles Mizrahi reminded me that in 1996, Warren Buffett issued a booklet entitled "An Owner's Manual.

While the purpose of the manual was to explain Berkshire's broad economic principles of operation, Charles Mizrahi believes that it is something special. It also contains important ideas that go beyond the Four Filters Formula to serve as guiding principles on how the company is run now and in the future. For understanding a wonderful business, this manual can serve us as a guide on what to avoid in a mediocre one.

Charlie Munger: "If you're going to buy something which compounds for 30 years at 15% per annum and you pay one 35% tax at the very end, the way that works out is that after taxes, you keep 13.3% per annum. In contrast, if you bought the same investment, but had to pay taxes every year of 35% out of the 15% that you earned, then your return would be 15% minus 35% of 15%—or only 9.75% per year compounded. So the difference there is over 3.5%. And what 3.5% does to the numbers over long holding periods like 30 years is truly eye-opening...." http://ycombinator.com/munger.html

From the 1985 Chairman's Letter.

A large portion of the realized gain in 1985 ($338 million pre-tax out of a total of $488 million) came about through the sale of our General Foods shares. We held most of these shares since 1980, when we had purchased them at a price far below what we felt was their per/share business value. Year by year, the managerial efforts of Jim Ferguson and Phil Smith substantially increased General Foods' business value and, last fall, Philip Morris made an offer for the company that reflected the increase.

We thus benefited from four factors: a bargain purchase price, a business with fine underlying economics, an able management concentrating on the interests of shareholders, and a buyer willing to pay full business value. While that last factor is the only one that produces reported earnings, we consider identification of the first three to be the key to building value for Berkshire shareholders. In selecting common stocks, we devote our attention to attractive purchases, not to the possibility of attractive sales.

(Note that General Foods is now a part of Kraft.)

GLOSSARY

Annual Report A report prepared by management that describes the financial condition and business operations which is distributed to all shareholders on a yearly basis.

Balance Sheet A financial statement that lists all the sources (namely, the liabilities and net worth) and uses (or assets) a firm has at the close of its accounting period.

Basis Point A basis point is 1/100th of 1%. So 50 basis points is 0.5%, 25 basis points is 0.25% and so on. Basis points make for a handy way to state small differences in yield. It is also used for interest rates. An interest rate of 5% is 50 basis points greater than an interest rate of 4.5%.

Bottom-up Approach A method of identifying investment opportunities one at a time through analysis of financial statements and the outlook of the company.

Beta   The risk of any individual share can be measured as the volatility of a share relative to the market as a whole. This ratio is known as the beta of a share. For standard reference, the entire market has a beta of 1.00, with a return corresponding to the market risk premium.

Bears   The bear attacks with a downward strike of the claws. They anticipate a falling market and they do their best to create one by selling and depositing cash in the money markets. Bears push prices down. And a market which falls over a sustained period is said to be a 'bear market'.

Bulls   The bull attacks with an upward strike of the horns. They anticipate a rising market and they do their best to create one by borrowing short term cash and buying. Bulls push prices up. And a market which rises over a sustained period is said to be a 'bull market'.

Bonds   A bond is a debt certificate establishing the debt of the borrower (the issuer) and his obligation to repay the lender (the investor) a fixed amount (the principal) on a specified future date (the maturity or redemption date).

Book Value   The difference between a company's assets and its liabilities, usually expressed in per-share terms. Book value is what would be left over for shareholders if the company was sold and its debt retired. It is calculated by subtracting total liabilities from total assets and dividing the result by the number of shares outstanding.

Business Cycle   The term, 'the business cycle', refers to a pattern of historically observed economic behavior whereby growth is cyclical.

Callable Bond   A bond which the issuer can decide to redeem before its stated maturity date. A call date and a call price are always given. You face a risk with a callable bond that it will be redeemed if its stated coupon is higher than prevailing rates at the time of its call date.

Capital Gains Tax   A tax on the increase in the value of assets - capital gains - realized in a given tax year.

Commercial Paper   Commercial Paper (CP) is short term unsecured debt issued by companies in the form of promissory notes as an obligation of the issuer. CP is typically issued at a discount to face value - but interest bearing notes can be requested. CP can be issued in bearer or registered form.

Commodity   Commodities are the raw materials used by industry and traded on specialist commodities markets. There are hard and soft commodities, soft being things such as cocoa, coffee, tea, sisal, sugar, soy, corn and pork bellies. Hard are metals, such as copper, tin aluminum etc. Commodities are dealt on a spot basis for immediate delivery and futures for later delivery.

Consolidation   This is when a company proportionally increases the nominal value of each share while decreasing the number of shares in the issue.

Convertible   A convertible is an adaptation of a straight bond issue which gives an investor the ability to convert the bond into a specified number of shares of the same issuer at a predetermined price.

Cost of Capital   The rate of return an enterprise has to offer to induce investors to provide it with capital. The cost of loan capital is the rate of interest that has to be paid. The cost of equity capital is the expected yield needed to induce investors to buy shares.

Derivatives   A derivative is a synthetic construction designed to give the same profile of returns as some underlying investment or transaction, without requiring the principal cash outlay. They derive their value from the performance of the underlying instrument.   Financial derivatives can be found in debt, equity, currency and commodity markets.

Dividend payout ratio The percentage of earnings paid in cash to shareholders. It is calculated by dividing the dividends paid by the earnings per share.

Dividend Yield   Dividend yield is found by dividing the latest known dividend payout from a company by its current share price. Dividend yield gives investors a figure for investment return in the form of income.

DJIA: An index of 30 stocks traded on the public exchanges. It is the most widely known index and is used as a measure of the health and direction of the overall stock market. Dow Jones Industrial Average "The Dow", or the "Dow Jones Industrial Average" (DJIA) is probably one of the best-known indices quoted in relation to the US equity markets. The index now consists of 30 stocks, and rather than dividing by 30, an adjusted index divisor is used to preserve continuity of the index over time through such events as stock splits, changes in the component stocks.

Earnings per Share (EPS) Pre-tax profits are divided by the amount of shares issued to get a figure for the amount of wealth that's been created per share by the company.

Economic Moat: A term coined by Warren Buffett referring to the competitive advantage a business has over its competitors. The moat acts as a barrier against other businesses trying to gain market share.

Efficiency of capital structures The debt: equity ratio suitable for a particular company will, to some extent, depend on the nature of that business. Generally speaking, low risk businesses can afford higher gearing than high risk businesses. Companies rarely make primary issues of shares, making use of debt markets for ongoing financing needs; and to attract debt finance, corporations must maintain their creditworthiness, which is in part determined by the debt: equity ratio.

Efficient market theory (EMT): a theory that states all information about a business is already reflected in the price of the stock, which is why one can not outperform the stock market.

Equity (stocks/shares) differs fundamentally from debt in two ways. It represents an ownership interest in a company – you're buying a share of the company, not lending the company money. A bondholder (basically, a lender) is entitled to a regular interest payment and can call for a winding up of the company if interest isn't paid. An equity holder is not entitled to any regular payment.

Footnotes: provides details for the numbers that appear in the company's financial statements. Supposed to provide a better understanding of a particular number.

Form 10-K: audited report filed annually with the Securities and Exchange Commission. Similar to the shareholder annual report but provides more detailed financial and non-financial information.

Free Cash Flow (FCF): the cash a business has after paying all its expenses and investing for its growth.

Frictional Costs   Frictional costs are the costs of doing a transaction (commissions, fees, brokerage, bid-offer spread).

Fundamental Analysis   Fundamental analysis looks at a share's market price in light of the company's underlying business proposition and financial situation. It involves making both quantitative and qualitative judgments about a company.

GDP   A country's Gross Domestic Product (GDP) is a measure of the total flow of goods and services produced over a specified time period, usually a year. The word 'gross' means that no deduction for the value of expenditure on capital goods for replacement purposes is made. Income arising from investment and possessions owned abroad is not included; and this distinguishes Gross Domestic Product (GDP) from Gross National Product (GNP).

Gearing Ratio   The ratio of debt to equity. The higher the ratio of debt to equity the more highly geared a company is said to be. The debt: equity ratio suitable for a particular company will, to some extent, depend on the nature of that business. Generally speaking, low risk businesses can afford higher gearing than high risk businesses.

Graham   Benjamin Graham developed a systematic approach to stock-picking by looking at a company's financial value before looking at market share price. Graham emphasized the need for careful selection. He learned the lesson of the 1920s speculative boom and bust frenzy and sought to inject rigor and foresight into what had previously been treated as a speculative arena. He was the author of Security Analysis, and the teacher of Warren Buffett at Columbia University.

High Yield Bonds   High yield bonds (formally known as 'junk bonds') are non-investment grade securities. They are debt instruments issued by corporations without a credit rating. The higher risk of default inherent with such securities means the issuer has to offer a higher return (higher yield) to compensate for the higher risk of default.

Inflation   An overall increase in the general price level. Where inflation is rising, even though some prices may fall, the overall cost of living and cost of business rises because most prices increase. The rate of inflation is the percentage change (usually annualized) in a price level index. Inflation reduces the real purchasing power of money.

Interest: (Compound Interest) is interest that is calculated on the basis of the principal sum plus any interest that has accrued. It pays interest on interest. The general formula for compound factor F for n years at an interest rate i is: $F_{n}, I = (1 + i)$ raised to the nth power.

Intrinsic Value   In the world of value investing, intrinsic value is the sum of all the free cash that can be taken out of a business during its lifetime that is discounted back to the present value, and divided by the number of shares outstanding. In the world of options, it is the difference between the exercise price of an option and the market value of the underlying instrument. Options at-the-money or out-of-the-money have no intrinsic value.

Investment Bank   Investment banks provide a range of financial and investment related services, advising clients on security issues, acquisitions and disposals of businesses, arranging and underwriting new issues, distributing securities and running fund management companies. They help make both the primary market and, through their trading desks and marketmakers, the secondary market.

LIBOR   Traditionally LIBOR (the London Interbank Offered Rate) has been defined as the rate at which a prime commercial bank is offered deposits by other banks in London. It is used as a measure of the cost of wholesale funds to banks and as a basis for pricing bank loans. LIBOR is an international reference rate and is used by the international market as a benchmark against which to price borrowing and lending.

Money managers: in return for a fee, persons responsible for buying and selling a portfolio of securities.

Mr. Market: a metaphor created by Benjamin Graham to demonstrate the erratic price swings of the stock market. Based on Mr. Market's "moods" he can be euphoric (bid prices higher) one day and be manic depressive (drive prices lower).

NASDAQ   The National Association of Securities Dealers Automated Quotation System) is the world's fourth largest stock market, behind New York, Tokyo and London. NASDAQ is a screen based market with over 500 marketmakers.

NIKKEI 225   The NIKKEI 225 Stock Average is a measure of share values on the Tokyo Stock Exchange. It is the simple average of the price of its 225 components with an adjustment made to take account of stock splits.

Net profit margin (NPM): A measure of how profitable a business is after all expenses and taxes are paid. Derive by dividing net income by total sales or revenue. Expressed as a percentage, it makes comparison between different businesses much easier.

On The Run   Bonds and notes most recently issued by the US Treasury. They are heavily traded and therefore tend to move at finer rates than other treasury securities.

Price/Book Ratio   The Price/Book ratio - also known as the 'price to net asset value ratio' - is a continuation of Net Asset Value analysis. This ratio gives an indicator of comparative – market against book – value.

PE ratio   A stock's market price divided by its current earnings per share. The PE Ratio is used by investors as a measure of the attractiveness of a particular security versus all other securities and their profit growth expectations.

PV ratio   This is the most important ratio for a value investor. A price lower than the intrinsic value help us insure a margin of safety in our purchase.

Proxy statement: information provided by management to shareholders so they can vote in an informed manner at annual shareholders' meetings. It also lists the total compensation paid to business executives.

Qualitative analysis Qualitative analysis uses nonnumeric factors to evaluate a business, its products, its competitive situation, and its managers to assess the business's prospects.

Quantitative Analysis Quantitative analysis is a form of analysis which uses numbers and ratios derived from a company's financials to assess its prospects.

Random walk theory: assumes that stock prices move randomly and unpredictably.

Return on equity (ROE): A measure of how profitable a business is. It is derived by dividing net income by total shareholder equity. ROE tells shareholders how effective management is in deploying their money. It is expressed as a percentage and makes comparison between different businesses much easier. However, consider that it can be affected by the level of debt employed by the company.

Risk   Value Investors view risk as simply risk of losing money. Academic Finance views risk is a measure of the variability of return. Thus, an investment where the return is guaranteed is less risky than an investment where returns are uncertain.

Risk Premium   The term 'risk premium' refers to the difference between the return attached to investments with different levels of risk.   The higher the risk taken, the higher is the return required to compensate for that risk.   The return offered by an investment should increase with the level of risk attached to that investment. The extra return component offered by higher risk investments is the risk premium.

Securities and Exchange Commission (SEC)   The federal agency responsible for oversight of publicly listed corporations, and for enforcing laws and regulations at the federal level.

S&P500 Index   The Standard & Poors 500 composite index. The index is a consolidation of other stock market indicators produced by the rating house Standard & Poors. Unlike the Dow, the S&P is a capitalization weighted index of 500 stocks chosen for market size, liquidity and industry group representation. It is one of the most widely used measures for US equity performance.

Top-Down Approach: a method of identifying investment opportunities by making a prediction about the future, determining the investment consequence and then selecting the proper security.

Transparency: disclosure of a company's financial reports so that investors can get a more accurate understanding of the financial condition of a company.

Underwriting A bank or underwriter guaranteeing to pay the issuer of securities a certain amount of cash for them. However this guarantee to buy the securities from the issuer and then resell them is risky. So, pricing an issue is important.
Value investing is a method of determining the value of a business and then buying shares at a discount from that value.

Yield The income from an investment expressed as a percentage of its price. Yield can be expressed in a number of ways, including: nominal yield, yield to maturity, and current yield.

The yield spread is the difference between the yield on one security and that of another.

Yield to Maturity   Yield to Maturity (YTM) is the interest rate that, if inserted in the DCF price equation, makes the given price of the bond exactly fair. It takes into account not only the cash flows coming from the bond, including any capital gain or loss at maturity, and also the timing.

Effective Yield of a Bargain Purchase after 10-years Chart.
From Mr. Bakul Lalla,[124]

Once you have a suitable investment candidate that fulfills the first three filters, estimate the intrinsic value. Using your estimated discount relative to market price, look to where the discount intersects with a reasonable growth rate to find an estimate for an effective yield after ten years.

Growth

Discounts	3%	4%	5%	6%	7%	8%	9%	10%	11%	12%	13%	14%	15%	16%	17%	18%	19%	20%
5%	3.53%	4.53%	5.54%	6.55%	7.55%	8.56%	9.56%	10.57%	11.57%	12.58%	13.58%	14.59%	15.59%	16.60%	17.60%	18.61%	19.61%	20.62%
10%	4.09%	5.10%	6.11%	7.12%	8.13%	9.14%	10.15%	11.17%	12.18%	13.19%	14.20%	15.21%	16.22%	17.23%	18.24%	19.25%	20.26%	21.27%
15%	4.69%	5.70%	6.72%	7.74%	8.75%	9.77%	10.79%	11.80%	12.82%	13.84%	14.85%	15.87%	16.88%	17.90%	18.92%	19.93%	20.95%	21.97%
20%	5.32%	6.35%	7.37%	8.39%	9.41%	10.44%	11.46%	12.48%	13.50%	14.53%	15.55%	16.57%	17.59%	18.62%	19.64%	20.66%	21.69%	22.71%
25%	6.01%	7.04%	8.06%	9.09%	10.12%	11.15%	12.18%	13.21%	14.24%	15.27%	16.30%	17.33%	18.36%	19.39%	20.41%	21.44%	22.47%	23.50%
30%	6.74%	7.78%	8.81%	9.85%	10.89%	11.92%	12.96%	13.99%	15.03%	16.07%	17.10%	18.14%	19.18%	20.21%	21.25%	22.28%	23.32%	24.36%
35%	7.53%	8.58%	9.62%	10.67%	11.71%	12.75%	13.80%	14.84%	15.89%	16.93%	17.97%	19.02%	20.06%	21.11%	22.15%	23.19%	24.24%	25.28%
40%	8.40%	9.45%	10.50%	11.56%	12.61%	13.66%	14.71%	15.77%	16.82%	17.87%	18.92%	19.97%	21.03%	22.08%	23.13%	24.18%	25.24%	26.29%
45%	9.35%	10.41%	11.47%	12.53%	13.59%	14.65%	15.72%	16.78%	17.84%	18.90%	19.96%	21.02%	22.08%	23.15%	24.21%	25.27%	26.33%	27.39%
50%	10.39%	11.46%	12.54%	13.61%	14.68%	15.75%	16.82%	17.90%	18.97%	20.04%	21.11%	22.18%	23.25%	24.33%	25.40%	26.47%	27.54%	28.61%
55%	11.56%	12.65%	13.73%	14.81%	15.89%	16.98%	18.06%	19.14%	20.23%	21.31%	22.39%	23.48%	24.56%	25.64%	26.73%	27.81%	28.89%	29.98%
60%	12.88%	13.98%	15.08%	16.17%	17.27%	18.36%	19.46%	20.56%	21.65%	22.75%	23.84%	24.94%	26.04%	27.13%	28.23%	29.32%	30.42%	31.51%
65%	14.40%	15.51%	16.62%	17.73%	18.84%	19.95%	21.07%	22.18%	23.29%	24.40%	25.51%	26.62%	27.73%	28.84%	29.95%	31.06%	32.17%	33.28%
70%	16.18%	17.31%	18.43%	19.56%	20.69%	21.82%	22.95%	24.07%	25.20%	26.33%	27.46%	28.59%	29.71%	30.84%	31.97%	33.10%	34.23%	35.35%
75%	18.32%	19.46%	20.61%	21.76%	22.91%	24.06%	25.21%	26.36%	27.51%	28.65%	29.80%	30.95%	32.10%	33.25%	34.40%	35.55%	36.70%	37.84%
80%	20.99%	22.16%	23.33%	24.51%	25.68%	26.86%	28.03%	29.21%	30.38%	31.56%	32.73%	33.91%	35.08%	36.26%	37.43%	38.61%	39.78%	40.95%
85%	24.52%	25.73%	26.93%	28.14%	29.35%	30.56%	31.77%	32.98%	34.19%	35.40%	36.61%	37.81%	39.02%	40.23%	41.44%	42.65%	43.86%	45.07%
90%	29.57%	30.93%	32.19%	33.45%	34.71%	35.96%	37.22%	38.48%	39.74%	41.00%	42.26%	43.52%	44.78%	46.04%	47.29%	48.55%	49.81%	51.07%

ENDNOTES

[1] The Four Filters, Berkshire Chairman's Letter to Shareholders, 2007.
[2] Berkshire Hathaway Annual Meeting, 2004.
[3] Charlie Munger talk at Harvard Law School, 2001.

[4] Berkshire Chairman's Letter to Shareholders, 2007, 6.

[5] Berkshire Chairman's Letter to Shareholders,

1989,(http://www.berkshirehathaway.com/letters/1989.html).

[6] Owner-oriented principles, Berkshire Hathaway Owner's Manual, 1996.
[7] Berkshire Chairman's Letter to Shareholders,

1989,(http://www.berkshirehathaway.com/letters/1989.html).

[8] (The Psychology of Human Misjudgment Revised Speech by Charles T. Munger), Kaufman, Peter D., Poor Charlie's Almanack, Virginia Beach, VA: PCA Publication, LLC, 2005.

[9] Charlie Munger's speech at USC Law School Commencement, 2007.

[10] Charlie Munger's speech at USC Law School Commencement, 2007.

[11] Berkshire Chairman's Letter to Shareholders, 1989,

(http://www.berkshirehathaway.com/letters/1989.html).

[12] A Lesson on Elementary, Worldly Wisdom As It Relates To Investment Management & Business". Charles Munger, USC Business School, 1994.

[13] Berkshire Chairman's Letter to Shareholders,

1994,(http://www.berkshirehathaway.com/letters/1994.html).

[14] Charlie Munger on checklists.

[15] Berkshire Hathaway Annual Meeting, 1995.

[16] Lowenstein, Roger, Buffett: The Making of an American Capitalist, New York, NY: Doubleday Dell Publishing Group, 1995

[17] Daniel Kahneman and Amos Tverksy, "Prospect Theory: An Analysis of Decision Under Risk," Econometrica, 47: 263-291 (1979).

[18] Takemura, K. (1992) Effect of decision time on framing of decision: A case of risky choice. behavior. Psychologia, 35, 180-185.

Takemura, K. (1994). Influence of elaboration on the framing of decisions. Journal of Psychology, 128, 33–39.

[19] Jim Rasmussen, "Billionaire Talks Strategy with Students," Omaha World-Herald, January 2, 1994, p.17S.

[20] Berkshire Chairman's Letter to Shareholders, 1999,(www.berkshirehathaway.com/1999ar/1999final.html)

[21] Labitan, C.,2003, unpublished masters project in Behavioral Finance, at Purdue University Calumet.

[22] Charlie Munger: USC Business School, 1994 Speech: A Lesson on Elementary, Worldly Wisdom As It Relates To Investment Management & Business.

[23] Charlie Munger: USC School of Law Commencement, May 13, 2007 .

[24] Charlie Munger: USC Business School, 1994 Speech: A Lesson on Elementary, Worldly Wisdom As It Relates To Investment Management & Business.

[25] Warren Buffett, University of Florida School of Business Speech October 15, 1998

[26] Berkshire Chairman's Letter to Shareholders, 1994.
[27] Berkshire Chairman's Letter to Shareholders, 1993.
[28] Charles T. Munger quote.
[29] Charlie Munger: USC Business School, 1994 Speech: A Lesson on Elementary, Worldly Wisdom As It Relates To Investment Management & Business.
[30] Berkshire Hathaway Annual Meeting, 2003.
[31] Buffett Partnership Letter, 1960.
[32] Berkshire Chairman's Letter to Shareholders, 1980.
[33] Berkshire Chairman's Letter to Shareholders, 1984.
[34] Berkshire Chairman's Letter to Shareholders, 1995.
[35] Berkshire Chairman's Letter to Shareholders, 1995.

[36] Hagstrom, Robert G., The Warren Buffett Way, Hoboken NJ: John Wiley & Sons, 1984.
[37] Berkshire Chairman's Letter to Shareholders, 1988.
[38] Berkshire Chairman's Letter to Shareholders, 1993.

[39] Warren Buffett, "The Superinvestors of Graham-and-Doddsville," Hermes (Fall 1984).
[40] Berkshire Chairman's Letter to Shareholders, 1993.
[41] Berkshire Chairman's Letter to Shareholders, 2001.

[42] From a talk given at the University of Florida, quoted in the Miami Herald (December 27, 1998), quoted in Kilpatrick, Of Permanent Value (2004), 1350.

[43] Berkshire Chairman's Letter to Shareholders, 1985.

[44] FORBES(1974), Warren Buffett Interview, 1974.

[45] Phil Fisher (mentioned in the Berkshire Chairman's Letter to Shareholders, 1988.) and Phil Carret (mentioned at the 1996 Berkshire Hathaway Annual Meeting). Both had outstanding investment records.

[46] The Psychology of Human Misjudgment by Charles T. Munger, Kaufman, Peter D., Poor Charlie's Almanack, Virginia Beach, VA: PCA Publication, LLC, 2005.

[47] Berkshire Chairman's Letter to Shareholders, 1992.
[48] Berkshire Chairman's Letter to Shareholders, 1981

[49] Charles Mizrahi quote

[50] http://www.forbes.com/business/forbes/2004/0426/142.html

[51] Berkshire Chairman's Letter to Shareholders, 1988.

[52] http://www.berkshirehathaway.com/ownman.pdf

[53] The New York Times Century of Business (Hardcover) by Floyd Norris and Christine Bockelmann, McGraw Hill, (Hardcover - Sep 23, 1999)

[54] Charlie Munger quote.

[55] The Psychology of Human Misjudgment by Charles T. Munger, Kaufman, Peter D., Poor Charlie's Almanack, Virginia Beach, VA: PCA Publication, LLC, 2005.

[56] Investing Principles Checklist, Kaufman, Peter D., Poor Charlie's Almanack, Virginia Beach, VA: PCA Publication, LLC, 2005.

[57] Warren Buffett, "What We Can Learn from Philip Fisher," Forbes (October 19, 1987).
[58] Berkshire Hathaway Annual Meeting, 2004.

[59] http://www.oid.com/public/html/CarretMemorial/CarretMem1.html

[60] J. K. Lasser's Pick Stocks Like Warren Buffett (Paperback) by Warren Boroson, Wiley, 2001.

[61] Frank Betz worked with Phil Carret. He is married to Phil's granddaughter Renee. They manage assets at the Carret/Zane Capital Management in Warren, New Jersey.
[62] Porter, Michael E., Competitive Advantage: Creating and Sustaining Superior Performance. Free Press, 1998.

[63] Warren Buffett, "The Superinvestors of Graham-and-Doddsville," Hermes (Fall 1984).

[64] A term used by successful Wall Street Trader, Michael Steinhardt.
[65] From a talk given at the University of Florida, quoted in the Miami Herald (December 27, 1998), quoted in Kilpatrick, Of Permanent Value (2004), 1350.

[66] Hagstrom, Robert G., The Warren Buffett Way, Hoboken NJ: John Wiley & Sons, 1984.

[67] Berkshire Chairman's Letter to Shareholders, 1995.
[68] Berkshire Chairman's Letter to Shareholders, 1989.
[69] Berkshire Chairman's Letter to Shareholders, 1981.
[70] Berkshire Chairman's Letter to Shareholders, 1982.
[71] Berkshire Chairman's Letter to Shareholders, 1993.

[72] Charles Mizrahi, "Getting Started in Value Investing", Hoboken NJ: John Wiley & Sons, 2006

[73] Morningstar.com,
http://quicktake.morningstar.com/stocknet/CashFlowRatios10.aspx?Country=USA&Symbol=KO

[74] Berkshire Chairman's Letter to Shareholders, 1991.

[75] Lowenstein, Roger, Buffett: The Making of an American Capitalist, New York, NY: Doubleday Dell Publishing Group, 1995

[76] Berkshire Chairman's Letter to Shareholders, 1991.
[77] Berkshire Chairman's Letter to Shareholders, 2001.
[78] Berkshire Chairman's Letter to Shareholders, 1990.
[79] Greenwald, Bruce and Kahn, Judd, Competition Demystified, New York NY: Penguin Group, 2005
[80] Michael E. Porter, Competitive Advantage: Creating and Sustaining Superior Performance (New York: The Free Press, 1985) p. 73.

[81] Value Investing: From Graham to Buffett and Beyond (Wiley Finance) by Bruce C. N. Greenwald, Judd Kahn, Paul D. Sonkin, Michael van Biema, 2001., p.75.

[82] Berkshire Chairman's Letter to Shareholders, 1989.

[83] Berkshire Chairman's Letter to Shareholders, 1996.
[84] Berkshire Chairman's Letter to Shareholders, 2007.
[85] "Able and honest people", Berkshire Chairman's Letter to Shareholders, 2002.
[86] Berkshire Hathaway Owner's Manual, www.berkshirehathaway.com/owners.html

[87] Berkshire Chairman's Letter to Shareholders, 1994.

[88] Robert Miles, The Warren Buffett CEO (Hoboken, NJ: Wiley, 2003).

[89] Berkshire Chairman's Letter to Shareholders, 1988.
[90] Berkshire Chairman's Letter to Shareholders, 1994.
[91] Berkshire Chairman's Letter to Shareholders, 1995.
[92] Berkshire Chairman's Letter to Shareholders, 1992.
[93] Berkshire Chairman's Letter to Shareholders, 1994.
[94] Berkshire Chairman's Letter to Shareholders, 2000.
[95] Berkshire Chairman's Letter to Shareholders, 1981.
[96] Berkshire Chairman's Letter to Shareholders, 1983.
[97] Berkshire Hathaway Owner's Manual, 1996.

[98] Barnett C. Helzberg, Barnett Helzberg, - What I Learned Before I Sold to Warren Buffett: An Entrepreneur's Guide to Developing a Highly Successful Company. Hoboken NJ: John Wiley & Sons ,2003

[99] Benjamin Graham Lecture Number Four, These lectures are from the series entitled Current Problems in Security Analysis that Mr. Graham presented at the New York Institute of Finance from September 1946 to February 1947. The book provides an abridged version of this content. The full text of the transcripts are contained within this website.
http://www.wiley.com/legacy/products/subject/finance/bgraham/benlec4.html
The Rediscovered Benjamin Graham: Selected Writings of the Wall Street Legend, by Janet Lowe.

[100] Berkshire Chairman's Letter to Shareholders, 1992.
[101] Berkshire Chairman's Letter to Shareholders, 1992.

[102] John Durr Williams, The Theory of Investment Value (Cambridge: Harvard University Press, 1938), pp. 186-91.

[103] Berkshire Chairman's Letter to Shareholders, 1992.
[104] Berkshire Chairman's Letter to Shareholders, 1992.

[105] Berkshire Chairman's Letter to Shareholders, 1992.

[106] Given this uncertainty, it's critical to buy stocks only when their valuation is so low that there's a huge "margin of safety," to use Ben Graham's famous saying. Consider this exchange from the 1996 Berkshire Hathaway (NYSE: BRK.A) annual meeting: "Warren talks about these discounted cash flows," said Vice Chairman Charlie Munger. "I've never seen him do one." "It's true," replied Buffett. "If [a company's value] doesn't just scream out at you, it's too close." A Valuation Rule of Thumb, article by Whitney Tilson (http://www.fool.com/news/foth/2001/foth010731.htm)

[107] Value Investing: From Graham to Buffett and Beyond (Wiley Finance) by Bruce C. N. Greenwald, Judd Kahn, Paul D. Sonkin, Michael van Biema, 2001

[108] Berkshire Chairman's Letter to Shareholders, 2007.

[109] Anton van Leeuwenhoek is generally recognized as an innovator in advancing the microscope, and pioneer of microbiology. (en.wikipedia.org/wiki/Anton_van_Leeuwenhoek)

[110] Daniel Kahneman and Amos Tverksy, "Prospect Theory: An Analysis of Decision Under Risk," Econometrica, (1979).

[111] Kaufman, Peter D., Poor Charlie's Almanack, Virginia Beach, VA: PCA Publication, LLC, 2005.

[112] Berkshire Chairman's Letter to Shareholders, 2007.

[113] Andrew Kilpatrick, Of Permanent Value: The Story of Warren Buffett (Birmingham, AL: AKPE, 1998), 683.

[114] Woolley, Suzanne, article in Money magazine: Mind Over Munger, July 1, 2002.
[115] Memos from the Chairman by Alan C. Greenberg, Workman Publishing Company, March 1, 1996.

[116] Berkshire Hathaway Annual Meeting, 2004.
[117] From the talk called "A Lesson on Elementary, Worldly Wisdom As It Relates To Investment Management & Business" by Charles Munger, USC Business School, 1994.
[118] Berkshire Chairman's Letter to Shareholders, 1996.

[119] Puri, Manju and Robinson, David T., "Optimism and Economic Choice" (May 2005). AFA 2006 Boston Meetings Paper Available at SSRN: http://ssrn.com/abstract=686240

[120] What is Value Investing?", Lawrence A. Cunningham, McGraw-Hill, March 12, 2004.

[121] Berkshire Chairman's Letter to Shareholders, 1977,

(http://www.berkshirehathaway.com/letters/1977.html).

[122] Berkshire Chairman's Letter to Shareholders, 1977.
[123] Berkshire Chairman's Letter to Shareholders, 1989.
[124] The Lalla Effective Yield After 10 Years Table, Based on a disscussion we had about the effect of a 50% bargain on a steady 7% earning company. Mr. Bakul Lalla expanded this idea and he was generous in donating this table to the MSN message board for BRK (http://groups.msn.com/BerkshireHathawayShareholders/messageboard.msnw). Bakul Lalla, a self-trained individual investor in Norwalk, California, has also been acknowledged in Michelle Leder's book "Financial Fine Print: Uncovering a Company's True Value."